"In every group effort, from athletics to tl[...] there is no single element more critical to success than strong and effective leadership. Identifying and explaining the broad range of qualities that comprise such a leader is no easy task. In *What Exceptional Leaders Know*, Wally Schmader and Tracy Spears meet this challenge by specifying, analyzing, and explaining each of the key characteristics of outstanding leadership. They use language that is clear and compelling, while providing the reader with a road map to becoming an exceptional leader him or herself."

-**Mike D'Orso**, *New York Times* best-selling author, winner of the Robert F. Kennedy Book Award, and six-time Pulitzer Prize nominee

"*What Exceptional Leaders Know* is a must-read book for anyone in a leadership position today. Whether in a corporation, faith based organization, government or not-for-profit organization, the tools and strategies you'll take from this book will be hugely valuable in your overall success."

-**Justin Sachs**, Author of *The Power of Persistence* and eight other best-selling titles

"Tracy Spears and Wally Schmader provide the reader with a blueprint for exceptional leadership. They help the reader understand what being a learning leader really means, and the crucial importance of humility. This book can transform your career."

-**Jim Stovall**, Best-selling author of *The Ultimate Gift* and many other titles

"Any company wishing to improve their bottom line should make the book, *What Exceptional Leaders Know*, mandatory reading prior to anyone being offered a management position. The book will be a wise choice for entrepreneurs as well. This book reveals smart leadership based upon the authors' many years of combined experience. Eliminate the "revolving door syndrome" in your business, buy the book!"

-**Elinor Stutz**, CEO of Smooth Sale, Author of *Inspired Business* and other best-selling books

"All leaders, whatever their career level, will find much to stimulate their thinking in this book. It will provoke thought and emotion as you uncover ways your actions,views, and choices shape your leadership. Leaders will be compelled to moveforward intentionally."

-**Amanda L. Smith**, MHA, CMPE, President, TenSmith LLC

"No one is more focused and intense in her zeal to deliver than Tracy Spears."

-**Phil Ross**, author, The Ross Organization

"Tracy Spears and Wally Schmader provide both emerging and established leaders with insightful leadership concepts presented in crystal clear and refreshingly simple ways. Readers will experience a number of "ah ha" moments that they can successfully translate into their professional, volunteer and personal lives. This book is a welcome and valuable addition to any leadership library."
                    -**Anna B. Goldenberg**, Principal, Goldenberg Consulting, LLC

"In *What Exceptional Leaders Know* Tracy Spears and Wally Schmader have compiled a plethora of resources and concepts for you add to your own leadership skill set. What Exceptional leaders Know will give you practical leadership coaching and help you to avoid some common leadership potholes."
                    -**Debra Wiggs**, Vice Chair MGMA, CEO Trinity Management Solutions

"Tracy Spears possesses and imparts superb insights to those she interacts with a leads. She was instrumental in sharing her perspectives, along with her team development and motivational skills."
                    -**Steve Richards**, President & CEO, Mood Media

"Wally Schmader has been a student of effective leadership for many years. He has packaged his best recommendations in a way that makes them easy for others to learn. These lessons are practical and get results."
                    -**Fortune Radio**

"Wally Schmader has very intriguing ideas. This kind of practical advice can be very hard to find."
                    -**Mike Mooslin**, CEO, CMM Enterprises

"After working with Tracy Spears, our staff is now functioning as a team with purpose and our sales have increased, even in this tough economy."
                    -**Sallie Hughes**, SR Hughes, Inc.

"Wally Schmader's unique and perspective allows him to combine the best of top-tier management and leadership studies with a "from the streets" approach, to make complex leadership and management topics accessible."
                    -**Ken Eissing**, President, North America, Mood Media

"What Tracy Spears delivers is not a run-of-the-mill workshop. We are a more cohesive group because of Tracy."
                    -**Bentonville Public Schools**

What Exceptional Leaders Know

High Impact Skills, Strategies & Ideas for Leaders

Tracy Spears & Wally Schmader

MOtivational PRESS®
LEADERS IN GLOBAL PUBLISHING

Published by Motivational Press, Inc.
7777 N Wickham Rd, # 12-247
Melbourne, FL 32940
www.MotivationalPress.com

Manufactured in the United States of America.

ISBN: 978-1-62865-136-2

Contents

Dedications

To Ronda, whose constant support I never take for granted. Thank you for your belief in me and your enthusiasm for this project. And to my Dad, whose definition of success influenced how I have decided to live my life.

-Wally

To Rosemary, for her support, for making me laugh every day, and for always picking me up at the airport. Thank you.

To my Parents, for a lifetime of lessons that served to push me to never be comfortable with the status quo.

-Tracy

A special thank you to all of the colleagues, mentors, coaches, thinkers, managers, trainers, good examples and bad examples who have influenced our understanding of what it means to be an exceptional leader.

-Wally & Tracy

Foreword

by Jim Stovall

No venture or organization can ever succeed and sustain success without leadership. The concept of leadership can seem elusive and mysterious because there have been so many books written, courses taught, and speeches made on the topic of how to be an effective leader. Unfortunately, many people purporting to tell you how to be a leader have never been one, nor have they studied, tested or quantified what makes a successful leader.

In my twenty-seven books, four motion pictures, hundreds of syndicated columns, and countless arena and corporate speeches, I have advised people to never take advice from those who don't have the experience or expertise to coach them. They need to find teachers and coaches who have accomplished what they hope to accomplish. Tracy Spears and Wally Schmader are these kinds of coaches. In these pages, they will present you with a blueprint for exceptional leadership. This blueprint can transform your career, but it is only as good as your willingness and motivation to apply the principles they present, and commit to becoming an exceptional leader yourself.

My late, great friend and mentor, Coach John Wooden, often told his players, "You will be known for a lifetime of great things you do or for one brief lapse in judgment." We are all aware of presidents, coaches, media stars, and icons of business who have lost their leadership, power, and position simply because they forgot that a leader is who they are, not what they do. Tracy and Wally will help the reader understand what being a learning leader really means, and the crucial role that humility will play over the course of your career.

We all had dreams and goals when we were teenagers or young adults. Then, all too often, those visions of greatness faded away. Some of us became so busy making a living that we forgot to create a life. I want you to understand that the biggest dreams you have ever had in your life are all still alive and well. They are ready to be activated, and that process can begin as you come to understand how to become an exceptional leader of your own life.

I want to encourage you to embrace the recommendations that Tracy and Wally are sharing with you within these pages. Stay connected to these lessons, understand them, and put them into action. They can lead you to your own sustainable success as an exceptional leader.

Let the journey begin.

Jim Stovall

2014

Introduction

Let's start with a few questions: Who was this book written for? What kind of leader will get the most value from it? Will it be worth your investment of time and money?

We have four target audiences for What Exceptional Leaders Know. They are:

1. The experienced leaders who feel that they could really use some fresh ideas and strategies to push themselves and their teams to the next level.

2. The new leaders who want to accelerate their skills and understanding of how exceptional leaders do their jobs.

3. The leadership coaches who want to keep current with what is working with leaders in the field, on the streets, and in the boardrooms.

4. Any leaders who think they may have peaked, that their most inspired days as managers or leaders may be behind them.

If you are in one of these groups, you are exactly the person we hope to reach with this book. We know you are serious about what you do and that you will absolutely benefit from learning what exceptional leaders know. As a progressive leader, you will have the opportunity to integrate these understandings into your own dynamic leadership skill set.

Try to think of a field or occupation where the levels of performance are as varied and disparate as they are among leaders. In the course of our working lives, almost all of us will work with leaders who are amazingly bad; some of us will work with leaders who are quite good, and a few of us will work with leaders who are exceptional.

Jim Collins calls these exceptional leaders "Level 5 Leaders." In the Six Sigma world, these leaders are "Black Belts." Robert Greenleaf said that the best leaders were "Servant Leaders." In a previous book, we referred to them as "Full Contact Leaders." Peter Drucker, Warren Bennis, Steven Covey, and Tom Peters described their attributes across many exceptional books. As any student of leadership knows, the traits of exceptional leaders appear again and again with different descriptions and labels to help us understand and assimilate them. So what are they?

We will be having this discussion in detail throughout this book. We will ask you some tough questions, ask you to re-think a few things, push you, inspire you, educate you, and provide real examples to illustrate our points. We will try to associate practical examples and recommended actions with the leadership traits we describe.

Let's begin by stating some crucial points many leaders have not yet considered. These are some of the aspects of exceptional leadership that many working leaders do not completely understand. They are truths that exceptional leaders know and that very few other leaders do:

Exceptional Leaders know that leadership is influence.

When you boil down everything a leader can do to succeed with a team, you end up with one word: influence. Exceptional leaders influence decisions, enthusiasm, actions, possibilities, confidence, beliefs, direction, and culture. Influence is what an exceptional leader does, and it shows up in myriad ways. The tactics can and will change; the definition will not.

Exceptional leaders know that leadership is not a talent.

Leadership is a skill and a craft. It can be learned only through a unique combination of study and experience. When people describe a "talented" leader or a "born leader", they're either mislabeling the leader's hard work or they're describing the leader's charisma. Of course, charisma and leadership are mistaken for each other very often, but they're not at all the same. Charisma is to leadership what a fresh paint job would be to a car. It can make for a more appealing presentation, but the actual performance will come from some deeper and more powerful place.

Exceptional leaders know how an understanding of personalities and temperaments allows them to succeed with different kinds of people.

We'll spend some time on this one because it's a real learning gap for a lot of us. It's amazing how much time leaders and managers spend thinking about incentives and promotions and how little we spend learning to understand temperaments and what motivates different kinds of people. A leader who does not study temperament theory will not be able to lead a broad group of diverse people. This will be the lid on their leadership potential. Do you know how to influence every type of person? Do you know what makes them tick? You will.

Exceptional leaders understand the power of words and phrases.

We cannot think of another crucial leadership skill that gets less attention than this one. A leader's ability to communicate effectively, express himself, and make his priorities known may be the most important skill of all. When we do reviews on leaders who were ineffective or unsuccessful in their roles, we are almost always describing a leader who did not know how to turn his expectations into words and phrases people would respond to. An inability to translate a vision or strategy into words that people can hear or understand can make a leader impotent. We will spend some time on this together.

Exceptional leaders are masterful storytellers.

Here is another example of where a leader's mastery of words will increase influence dramatically. This is one of the few aspects of leadership that some people seem to understand naturally, but most of us need to learn how to do it.

Exceptional leaders understand that they're a work in progress.

The best leaders, the most effective leaders, and the leaders with the most upside all get this. We all need to see ourselves as people who are actively improving. We are learning leaders, we are observers, and we are students. Show me a leader who thinks he or she has nothing to learn, and I will show you someone who will be obsolete in a matter of a few years (if not already). This is a persistent misunderstanding of ineffective leaders; they just don't understand that when you quit working on yourself, you're admitting that you have no upside. The work-in-progress leader is an attractive leader who will gather skills, insights and followers very quickly. This is you.

Exceptional leaders trust their instincts and do not always give in to consensus or popular opinion.

This can be a tough one. Top leaders know when a situation calls for a consensus and when a simple decision from the leader is needed. If a leader repeatedly gets this wrong, he can work very hard and get almost nothing done. We will discuss how to manage through these decisions.

Exceptional leaders know the difference between leadership and manipulation.

The Difference Between Leadership and Manipulation could be a book unto itself. A lot of the "leadership" executed by non-developed leaders is actually just some form of manipulation. There's a time for both, but it's crucial to understand the difference and to know what you're doing. Manipulation can be used successfully and honestly by a leader who understands that it's a short-term strategy. It cannot take the place of a real purpose or mission for your team. Developed leaders can discern what their teams need and when they need it. They make strategic decisions that will not put their credibility or long-term goals at risk.

Exceptional leaders know that what people want most is very easy to give them.

This one you know already. People want to be understood, engaged, energized, and recognized. There are lots of ways to do this, and we will discuss a number of them.

Exceptional leaders understand the importance of self-awareness.

This is the only leadership trait on this list that often gets worse for leaders with lots of experience. New leaders are often too self-aware, and this self-awareness naturally recedes to a healthy (and effective) level with time. Experienced leaders, though, can totally lose touch with the crucial importance of self-awareness. There are experienced leaders who never even consider how they're being perceived or the impact they may be having on their teams. In the worst cases, this lack of understanding can undo a lot of good work and severely stunt the leader's effectiveness. We'll dig into this one to show how to avoid that outcome.

Exceptional leaders understand that they're thermostats, not thermometers.

The best leaders know that they're responsible for the environment. They're not just there to quantify and understand what is happening with their teams or organizations; they exist in their roles to create and maintain a high-performance environment. The thermometer is there to tell the temperature, but the thermostat is there to set the temperature. Max DePree said it best: "The first responsibility of a leader is to define reality." That reality is a complex mixture of personalities, objectives, and challenges. Exceptional leaders know that it's their privilege to influence these variables in lasting and meaningful ways.

Throughout the book we will have ☑**WELK**notes where we distill ideas from a chapter into one or two-line notes to help readers remember high-impact ideas. WELK stands for What Exceptional Leaders Know, and these notes can help organize important takeaways from the book.

Let's get started.

Exceptional Leaders Are Self-Aware

Chapter 1 - What Are You Known For?

There are very few topics so important that they are the sum total of *everything* you do through your career. The total of your successes, your failures, your promotions, your initiatives, your hard work, your collaborations, your decisions … all of it adds up to your reputation.

A lot goes into a career, a lot of time, a lot of change, and a lot of work. You invest an immense amount of yourself into your career, especially as a leader. Your reputation is the only thing you will really get to keep for all of the work you do. The titles will go away, the money you earn will be spent, your responsibilities will eventually be given to someone else, but you will keep your reputation.

What is your professional reputation? What are you known for? This can be one of the more difficult questions to answer objectively, but most of us have a pretty good idea about our own reputations.

If I were to ask your direct reports what it's like to work for you or with you, what would they say?

What is the *best* thing about your professional reputation at this point in your career?

What is the *worst* thing about your professional reputation at this point in your career?

Most of us believe that our reputations are fair and well-deserved, and some of us have been careful to pay attention to what we are becoming known for over the course of our careers. What about the rest of us?

Reputations, good or bad, are sturdy constructions that take a lot of time to make and even more time to change. We have all had the jarring experience of having someone describe us or deal with us in a way that does not match how we see ourselves. It can be really shocking when someone else's view of you drastically contradicts your own self-image. These scenarios make for effective wake-up calls for many of us. Reputations can also be very fragile, changing drastically with one crucial misstep. It happens every day.

What would you like your reputation to be?

This is a big question because reputation is such a big thing, and it's important to answer it honestly. For many people, reputation is an accident because it's left to chance. Even professionals with excellent overall reputations are unlikely to have spent much forethought on the idea of what they actually wanted to be known for.

It wasn't until a few years ago when progressive business thinkers began talking and writing about the concept of "personal branding" that most professionals began to realize that they, like any other commercial product, have a brand. In fact, they actually *were* a brand, and at the base of that personal brand was *reputation*.

Using branding to understand reputation is a great way to recognize that building a great reputation is a process. Everyone understands what companies do to build a brand. They understand how long and how much effort it takes for a brand to mean what the creators hope it means, and they understand that a brand can be fragile.

- The New York Times
- Rolex
- Chik-Fil-A
- Exxon
- Facebook

- Apple
- Kanye West
- Wal-Mart
- Tesla
- Martha Stewart
- Bill Gates
- McDonald's
- Hyundai
- George W. Bush
- Monsanto
- Tony Romo
- Audi
- Kodak
- Reddit
- Andy Warhol
- Tylenol
- Kobe Bryant
- CNN
- Citibank
- Richard Branson
- Alec Baldwin
- General Motors
- The Boston Red Sox

Did you notice that there's no separation between the brand name and the associated reputation? Did you also notice that, in some cases, you were immediately aware of a "brand story" or background information that may have influenced the current evaluation of the person or brand?

The lesson here is that brands, both personal and commercial, are dynamic. They are always in flux, always being created and reformed.

Is there a gap between how you're known today and how you would like to be known?

This is the opportunity question. That gap is where you find ambition and your professional upside as a leader. That aspirational space between who you are today as a leader and who you would like to be is where exceptional leaders spend a lot of time. Any improving reputation or brand needs to be curated over time. It's very hard work because your reputation is the sum total of everything you are and do.

The big question is: How do you *curate* an amazing reputation? Answer: By understanding all of the elements that going into making one. Let's start with humility, which is one of the key building blocks of your reputation.

☑WELKnote:

Your reputation is your brand. It is one of your most valuable assets as a leader. Protect it.

Chapter 2 - Humility and Leadership

What is the most attractive personality trait for a leader? Confidence? A positive attitude? Focus? Enthusiasm? Charisma?

You could make a pretty good case for any of these traits, and most effective leaders have at least a few of them. Of course, there's a whole other discussion about what makes a leader attractive to his or her team. These characteristics will often be quite different from the traits that would make him valuable to his bosses. For now, let's focus on what makes a leader attractive and engaging to the team she's leading, the team she's responsible for.

Lots of management and leadership books attempt to explain the stages of a leader's development. It's a tricky business, because while we know that effective leaders do graduate through stages as they gain understanding and experience, we also know that these stages differ for all of us based on what innate characteristics we bring to the job.

Are you a naturally good communicator? Are you ultra-competent in your industry? Have you always been empathetic? Are you quick-witted?

These are characteristics that could define you as a leader. We tend to lead with our strongest base-line character traits when we first become leaders. It's our go-to characteristic, and along with the personality mix we described previously, it makes us who we are as a leader. For now, let's think about these outward personal traits as being kind of a default setting for ourselves as leaders. Like being right-handed or speaking English, you don't have to think about them ... they're just you.

Many leaders never move past their basic leadership personae. They are who they are, and with no intervening influences, they will stay who they are. It would be easy to make a list of all of the "tells" that clearly mark leaders who have not developed themselves, leaders who present themselves to their teams "as is."

You know them when you work with them. You may even be able to see how much more they could be in their role as a leader, but you don't want to be one of them. One great thing about writing books like this one is that your audience selects themselves. Only people who want to improve personally and as and leaders will ever pick up this book. We know you're not in that "as is" category of leaders because you would not be reading these words. The idea that you know you can improve is a demonstration of your confidence and high self-esteem. You're to be congratulated.

So let's get back to that first question. What is that single high-level trait that is at the foundation of all great leaders' personalities? Humility.

Think about it for a moment. Humility is the trait that opens a leader up to everything else. Humility is what allows us to know that we can improve and influence. Humility is at the very top of the list of high-level leadership characteristics. Look at how we can use humility to improve ourselves and become more influential to the people around us.

We should define humility and maybe the opposite of it as well. Most of the common definitions of humility talk about (1) lowering one's self in relation to others and (2) having a clear perspective, and therefore an implicit respect, for another person's place. We could probably all agree that the opposite of humility would be an inability to lower one's self or to "peer" with someone you perceived to be less important, or less accomplished.

We need a shift in perspective for any of us to approach our full potential as leaders. It's a difficult shift in perspective, and it's a shift decidedly in the direction of humility. To be a truly effective leader, you must truly value the people on your team and literally go to work for them. In *The Art of Leadership*, Max De Pree tells us that leaders should see themselves as "servants" of their people in that they remove the obstacles that could prevent them from doing their best work.

This kind of humility is not often found in leaders. Most of us actually found our way into leadership positions because of our ego drive. To earn the kind of trust and belief you will require to drive peak performance with your team, you will need to develop this kind of leadership humility. It's one of the non-negotiable philosophical underpinnings of true leadership.

So how do you get there? How do you develop the kind of humility that shows your staff that you really understand your role and respect theirs? It starts with an acknowledgement of who works for whom. This kind of acknowledgement in an organization does a lot of good. It sets a very democratic tone without an attempt to sell your team on a participative management model that everyone knows is not going to happen. Being democratic does not mean the leader is not accountable for direction and results. Truthfully acknowledging who works for whom also breaks down the fictional and debilitating "everybody works for the boss" idea.

In my first leadership role as a district sales manager in Raleigh, North Carolina, I had a small team comprised mostly of young college graduates. We were all about the same age. The only thing distinguishing me from my team was my title and some experience with the company. At first, I tried to use that title to manufacture productivity. Like most young leaders, I enjoyed my title and imagined that it was a very important difference between "my" team and me. It did not take long for me to realize that managing by title creates a "please the boss" environment that is often not productive at all. It caused all sorts of problems: different levels of productivity when I was there than when I wasn't, gossip and people "telling" on each other, and the errant belief that their job security was mostly rooted in their relationships with me. All of these were serious impediments to productivity.

I decided to have my first "who works for whom" meeting. We all sat down and after a short discussion came to understand our real roles and responsibilities. They realized that, as commissioned salespeople, they worked for their prospects and clients, not for their sales manager. The prospects and clients paid their bills and would make the final decision about whether they succeeded as sales people or not. We also realized that I, as the leader, actually worked for them. I was literally paid by them (overrides on their commissions) and would succeed or fail as a leader based on their productivity. Isn't that true even if there isn't an "override"? There was no way around it; I worked for them. This understanding was a big step for me as a leader. I could either embrace the truth and use it to move my organization forward, or I could stick with my ego drive and force my team to play along with my fictional sense of superiority.

This leadership superiority conceit has been responsible for much of the distance between leaders and their people. This "authority gap" is unnecessary and a presents a real productivity risk to your organization. It can block the flow of trust and ideas between you and the members of your team who will be responsible for getting the important work done.

How do you eliminate this gap and move your team in the direction of trust and interdependence? Here is a short list of simple changes and ideas I recommend for closing this gap:

- Share problems and issues with your team. Be transparent, it shows your confidence in your people. Give the news and be confident there's a solution. Don't be afraid of bad morale. Nothing is worse for morale than the collective sense that you're not sharing important information. Assume that they value their jobs and roles just as much as you do. Transparency is your ally in building trust.

- Keep your door open. Unless the conversation is absolutely private, there's no reason for closed-door conversations in business. We are all here to succeed. It also perpetuates some kind of paranoia people instinctively have that they're the subject of the closed-door conversation.

- Humility can mean a lot of things. Small acts mean a lot. Make the coffee, leave the best parking spot for someone else, open the door for them, make sure someone's chair is comfortable, work in the common work areas. Don't always think your story is most important, don't "one-up" people under any circumstances. You're the boss. You probably get paid more. That is enough.

- Surprise people with involvement. Ask opinions about issues outside of their responsibility. It shows people you don't always think you have the best answers. Guess what? You don't.

- Think about the ways you hold yourself above your team. Then think about the reasons why. Challenge yourself and make some changes where you can. They all count.

False Humility

Humility is not lowering yourself to others; it's raising others up to your level. It's leveling the playing field. Falsely "lowering" yourself or placating someone is as off-putting as bad personal hygiene. People can immediately smell it and will move to the other room as quickly as possible.

I'm sure you have experienced this situation before. You say, "That was a great blog. I really loved what you had to say!" only to hear in response, "I really didn't like how that turned out." I have been on the golf course and complimented a long drive, then received the response, "I used to hit it much longer." What are you supposed to say back to that? Why is it that a well-intentioned compliment sometimes turns into you actually trying to "sell" the recipient on it, or be forced to re-compliment them?

Worse yet are the people who are "fishing" for a compliment. They ask a question or make a comment to get people to talk about how amazing *they* are.

We all know that this is just someone's insecurity coming out, but that doesn't make it any more attractive. The next time you catch yourself feeling exposed by something nice that has been said, say "Thank you." It's that simple. No need to go on and on or justify the compliment. I'm warning you that it won't be easy, but it will be obvious to you when it happens. This is part of the personal growth work that is needed to become authentically humble.

Making a decision to develop yourself into a high-performance leader requires a detachment from ego and the embracing of humility. It means relating to your staff as peers who just have different responsibilities to the organization. This kind of democratic team, free from the constraints of ego and position, will always out-perform a traditional boss-subordinate arrangement over the long term.

Developed leaders know that their own personal humility combined with all of their other dynamic traits makes them much more effective at influencing team performance. This overt embrace and development of personal humility will give you much more potential and upside as a leader. It will actually push up your leadership lid and make it easier for you to engage and influence different kinds of people. The bottom line is that humility is a cornerstone character trait for every exceptional leader.

☑WELKnote:

Genuine humility is the most attractive leadership personality trait ... and it can be learned.

Chapter 3 - The Last to Know

Most leaders pride themselves on being in the know and current with what is happening in their companies, in their industries, and in their own areas of responsibility. Leaders and managers are usually the first people everyone goes to for information. This is what makes this next sentence so ironic. Leaders are usually the very last to know about their own limitations and liabilities.

You were given leadership responsibilities because you're competent and you have real skills and experience. You were the person who knew how to do it best, right? So why is it that leaders themselves are often the last to become aware of their own individual shortcomings in their roles?

There are many reasons for this. For one, most companies do not do 360° leadership reviews. Most leaders do not take the initiative to ask their teams for suggestions on how they can improve. Additionally, very few companies cross-train their teams so that managers get to do other people's jobs to understand what they really need from leadership. Even very smart leaders can be egocentric and believe they have a handle on what their teams need and expect from them. In many cases the leaders' jobs have changed over time, and what they used to be really good at just doesn't count for as much anymore. The truth is that most leaders do not have an accurate view of themselves as seen through the eyes of their people.

We all know that the road to obsolescence for a leader has become much shorter over the last ten years. The acceleration of workplace technology and virtual working relationships has created a whole new set of skills that truly effective leaders need to master. The mandatory skills are changing; the obstacles are changing; even business vocabulary is changing. If a leader is not staying ahead of all of this or at least keeping up, it will be obvious to everyone. First, this will be obvious to the leader's team, and then over time it will become obvious to the leader's bosses. Many of today's tenured leaders are responding to these changes with denial instead of development, and it won't work.

The bottom line? As a leader, if you're trying to lead in today's workplace with yesterday's skills, ideas, or strategies, you won't be a top performer. It's as simple as that.

When companies hire management consultants, we often see a lot of attention paid to "position tenure," looking closely at how long the leaders in a certain company have been in their roles with the same people reporting to them. The results of these studies are almost always the same: Businesses where the same leaders have been in the same roles with the same people reporting to them over a long period of time typically do not grow. There are different reasons for this, of course, but it's usually simple stagnation. These leaders are not learning new things, and they do not have to improve themselves to retain their roles. Their teams know a few crucial things about them:

- They know what the leader is going to say and do in most situations.
- They know how the leader is going to react in most circumstances.
- They know the leader's habitual response to pressure.
- They understand the leader's expectations.
- They know what the leader is, and isn't, going to take responsibility for.

A predictable leader can become nearly muted and nearly invisible. If everyone already knows what she's going to do and say, what's the point of even saying or doing it? Obsolescence has a predictable rhythm, and it starts with leaders believing that they do not have to keep working on themselves.

Here's the good news: There's a LOT we can do to avoid this situation, even if you've been in the same role for a long time. It starts with self-awareness and not thinking you're above the idea of getting better over time. If you're being paid to lead, and you have people above and below you on the org chart expecting your best, you have an obligation to perform. Part of this obligation is the concept of personal and professional development. Don't you want to be the leader who surprises people with new ideas and fresh approaches? Isn't it in your interest to make sure that your best and most vital days as a leader are ahead of you? Let's make a commitment to that idea together.

☑WELKnote:

Leaders must actively defend themselves against obsolescence.

Chapter 4 - Becoming Your Own Turn Around CEO

If I were to come into your business or your group, what would be the first thing I would change? I'm asking you because I want you to think again. I'm not insinuating you're not smart; I'm implying you're probably on autopilot and not thinking as creatively as you did when you first took the position, operating more from a micro level instead of a macro level.

I get it. You were hired to lead the team. In the beginning, you spent day and night trying to "right the ship." You worked insane hours and weekends. You made a bunch of necessary changes. You brought in a few of your own people to help. You made an amazing amount of progress, and then it happened.

Things are finally calm. Everyone finally knows the direction you're heading. You're in a rhythm with them. They know how you will respond without even asking. On Monday, you walk into your office, say hello to a few of the staff, sit down, start returning emails, and dial in to the first of many conference calls for the day. Maybe throw in a few meetings, have some lunch, and before you know it, it's 6:00 and time to go home, only to do it all again tomorrow ... and the next day ... and the next day.

Some of you are reading this and wondering what the issue is with this kind of day. This is your job. This is what you were hired for. Right?

If this sounds familiar, consider this. Returning emails, jumping on conference calls, and putting out fires is not why you were promoted or hired. You could explain that all of the busy stuff is important, but it may not actually be moving your business forward at all.

Imagine you were the best conference call participant, report reviewer, and email responder in the world, the best who'd ever lived. Fast forward ten or twenty years. What have you done? Business should be about DOING things, things that you care about, things the customer can see and feel, and things that make people glad to be on the team.

Though some of these duties are part of your job description, they're not the only things the organization wants or needs from you. They need your brains, your vision, your ability to connect with employees, your excitement, and your experience. Simply stated, they need your best.

When was the last time you did not look at your emails all day on a workday? Or weren't on conference calls all day? Vacation days don't count. Which reminds me, when was the last time you took a vacation? No, not the kind where you're checking your phone every few minutes. I'm talking about a real vacation, one that requires a little planning, a hotel, and maybe even a plane to get there.

We all do it. We say something like, "It's just easier for me to check in every day so I'm not bombarded when I get back," or this one: "If I don't respond, I might hold a project or contract up." Doesn't that make you feel important? The real truth is that someone else in your company could probably do those things while you're out.

So quit thinking you must oversee every single thing. Being a micro manager doesn't do anyone any good. It burns out the best of leaders and frustrates most of your employees anyway. As if that's not reason enough to stop, there's an equally bigger down side to not delegating to others. You rob your people of the opportunity to grow and of the opportunity to contribute. Often, micro managers say things like, "It's just easier to do it myself," or, "I don't have time to walk them through it."

Make time. It might take more time once or twice, but if that person can learn to handle that situation every time it comes up over the lifetime of their employment, don't you think ultimately it will actually save a *lot* of time?

This might be the one strategy you like best in this book. Take a vacation every quarter. Completely detach from the business. Leave behind the laptop and the cell phone. Don't dial into that one call you just can't miss. Be present in your vacation and take the time to recharge your battery. You'll return with a fresh perspective again. You will also be more creative, more rested, more focused, more likeable, and yes, a better leader. So where will you be going this quarter?

☑WELKnote:

Exceptional Leaders are constantly reinventing themselves... they do not coast.

Chapter 5 - How Exceptional Leaders Manage Stress

Managing stress as a leader is critical. Leaders do not have the luxury of being grumpy or volatile in front of their people. Those are indulgences that you can no longer claim when you're charged with leading people. Many people will never become truly effective leaders or have responsibility for others simply because they cannot hold themselves together well enough to be reliable for other people.

It's not possible to eliminate stress from your world, so the only constructive way to approach the topic is to examine where personal stress comes from and then reflect on ways of managing it. For most leaders, stress comes from three distinct sources. Studying these sources is the first step in learning how to deal with it positively. For many leaders, simply figuring out where their personal stress is coming from helps them to manage it. A feeling of control over daily pressure and stress is rooted in an understanding of ourselves and how we imagine stressors.

"Locus of control" is a term for the extent to which individuals believe they can control events that affect them. Individuals with a high internal locus of control believe that events in their life derive primarily from their own actions. For example, when receiving test results, people with an internal locus of control tend to praise or blame themselves and their abilities, whereas people with an external locus of control tend to praise or blame an external factor such as the teacher or the test.

External Locus of Control in Leaders

Having an external locus of control describes a person who looks outward for approval and recognition. This person may be a very capable person in every way and, over time, may develop a need for outside approval in order to feel good about herself or the job she's doing. This person generally works very well in group or team environments and can be an excellent collaborator. She's coachable and respectful of the "chain of command" in the organization.

Internal Locus of Control in Leaders

Having an "internal" locus of control means that the person's sense of accomplishment, success, and capability comes from the inside. These people tend to be wary of positive recognition and are not always the best collaborators. They're usually good organizers and successful lead-from-the-front managers where their credibility can be seen clearly.

Many leaders develop an external locus of control over time because they need to satisfy so many people. This is where having an external locus of control can make it hard to become an exceptional leader. When you consider the leader's need to be sensitive to his team, to perform for his bosses, to be attentive to his partner, and to have quality time with his kids, it's easy to see where stress comes from. Keeping all of these different people satisfied can be very challenging.

Because of this, many leaders begin to feel good about themselves to the extent that they can please others, thus developing an external locus of control. A good way to tell how people are psychologically constructed is to ask the simple question, "How do you know when you've done a good job?"

First responses will indicate an internal or external locus of control. If they say, "I know because I feel good about myself," or "I feel proud to have accomplished something," they're self-satisfiers who are able to feel successful without other people telling them they're successful. On the contrary, if the question is answered with something like, "When my boss is impressed," or, "I get recognized," or "I earn my bonus," then you know they want the outside world to tell them they're successful.

As leaders, care should be taken with this because either extreme can cause problems. Think about where your personal locus of control is. Is this way of thinking helping you as a leader? Is it something you may need to change over time? Exceptional leaders understand that most of the improvement they make will happen on the inside and be reflected and magnified in their relationships with people. They are not afraid to examine themselves and look for areas that could improve, and this trait gives them ultimate credibility with their teams and peers.

Another way to gauge whether a leader has been overstressed is when a kind of leadership roleplaying sets in, and it's a problem for experienced leaders more than new leaders, especially for a leader who has worked with the same people over a long period of time.

This roleplaying mode can set in when the passion and excitement a leader has for his opportunity or his team begins to fade. This stressed leader starts to use a kind of pretend enthusiasm. He begins to hear himself saying the right things in the right way, but with a kind of detachment. The leader's overall disposition and personality do not change, but he's going about his job without passion and emotional engagement. Any leader who has ever felt this will recognize it when he sees it in someone else. It's not that the leader is being careless: He just actually does care less than he used to.

What can we do about it if we're in this mode?

First, we have to understand that all adults develop a veneer over their real and original personalities that allow them to get along with and satisfy the people in their lives. This veneer is both necessary and inevitable, and it's an important part of the polite society, but it's not actually you, who you are on the inside.

There's an Italian term from the art world called *pentimento*. The word describes a process that occurs over time in oil paintings where the artist's previous attempts on the canvas begin to show through. Over a period of many years, the original painting starts to become visible and eventually even overtakes the final painting.

That original painted-over image is your true and best self. Over time, a leader's real persona will come to the surface just as in the old paintings. That person does not rely on popularity or satisfying others to feel good. He feels good because he's good and he's doing his best with his people. This is the exceptional leader who knows he is a work in progress and is actively improving as a professional.

What are some other stressors that can affect our ability to lead successfully?

Feeling That You Are Doing Less Than You Can

Another big source of stress among high achievers and leaders is the idea that they're doing less than they can. Most leaders consider themselves to be highly capable performers who can produce at a high level all of the time. Realistically, this is almost impossible to do. Many leaders put intense pressure on themselves to perform at an incredibly high level all the time without making any compromises. It's this prototypical highly ambitious and competitive A-type leader who is most likely to experience the kind of stress that comes from being unrealistic about her capability.

A person cannot be "on" all of the time. It's not even in a leader's best interest to try. Leadership is about balance and knowing when it's time to turn things up and when it's time to use the brakes. Deliberately slowing yourself down can be one of the hardest things to do. The leader must understand that every meeting is not "the" meeting, every month is not "the" month, and every presentation is not "the" presentation. Exceptional leaders have real perspective and learn that the ability to demonstrate this balanced perspective is as important for their followers as it is for themselves.

In managing an organization, you'll have a thousand little "moments of truth" each week, and it's important to be able to differentiate them. Listed below are a few areas of confusion that can knock an otherwise capable leader out of balance if he doesn't know the difference between:

- Busyness and productivity
- Hard work and performance
- Completion and accomplishment
- Being highly motivated and being hyperactive

Your people depend on you to model both goal-orientation and balance. Sometimes that means pulling back on the accelerator a bit. Allow yourself to do this, and your team's overall performance will increase while your personal stress level decreases.

Thinking about Yourself Too Much

"The greatest cause of stress is thinking too much about yourself." I remember where I was the first time I heard that sentence. It was at a leadership seminar outside of Atlanta in the mid-1990s. The topic under discussion was stress and where it comes from. I didn't accept this statement at first. I simply wrote it in my journal to consider later.

I've thought about it many times since then, and I eventually realized that it's absolutely true. It's become almost fashionable to be "stressed out" and to say so when someone asks you how you're doing. It's definitely a narcissistic comment because it then falls to the asker to query, "Really? Why?" Then the stressed person gets to list his unique challenges and issues.

Why isn't being calm, peaceful, and serene fashionable? It should be, but instead, everyone wants to report being busy and stressed. As a leader, you have to think clearly about what is actually going on. It's true–stress is caused by thinking about one's self. Things are not going the way you hoped they would go; you have not had enough time to do something you want to do; you're stressed because the month is looking bad, etc. A leader cannot get tangled up in this kind of thought and still be responsive to his team and his family.

Simple worry is the biggest root of stress, both justifiable worry that your condition will worsen in some way and the kind of fictional worry that centers on things that will never happen.

Earl Nightingale said, "Worry is the misuse of the imagination." I believe that most stress could fall under that same definition. The best way to escape from self-centered stress is to get busy doing things for other people. Actively seek out people in your organization to help and teach and pull your attention away from your own condition. Feelings of stress and expressions of stress are not going to help anything anyway. We all have legitimate worries that should be taken seriously, but the rest of what we call stress is just noise, and it's not going to go away. The best course of action may be to make a positive impact on as many people as you can. If we can do this as leaders, at least the noise will be much harder to hear.

☑WELKnote:

Stress is going to be part of every leader's job. Understanding where it comes from and how to manage it is a key step in becoming an exceptional leader.

Chapter 6 - Bifocal Leadership

Why have traditional "people skills" fallen by the wayside in many organizations? And why does that represent a special opportunity for us?

It used to be that a person rose in a corporation according to how far his work ethic, necessary technical competency, and people skills would take him. The work ethic piece is still necessary and technical skills may be more important than ever, but the people skills part of this traditional skill set is no longer prioritized in many businesses. Why?

In today's businesses, more key executives have risen from technical or finance/accounting roles than ever before. Paying attention to trends in executive succession lines has always been a great way to judge what is being valued in the business world. There was a time when most key executives rose from the sales ranks. Today your president or CEO is more likely to be an accountant or IT person. That does not necessarily mean that they don't have people skills; in fact, most do. It means their management biases will usually go in the direction of the executive expertise. In the accountant's/executive's case, she will most likely manage through and with the numbers. The IT expert will also be more likely to make decisions in the direction the data points her. With the easy access we all now have to great reports and meaningful metrics, many organizations have become extremely data-driven. Some experts are now beginning to identify the risks of making too many important decisions using raw data, but most leaders are not listening yet.

The implications of the "letting the data tell us what to do" model can be scary. This is where a lack of soft leadership skills like discernment and vision can create a lot of risk for a business or organization.

Each successive generation of business people wants to assign a couple of myths to their particular era. It's important to understand these myths and expose them for what they are.

Myth #1: There's more competitive pressure than ever.

False. There has always been intense competitive pressure. Yes, we have international competitive pressure, but with it comes a correspondingly larger market to sell to. Interlopers have always been there. Competition has always existed, both priced competition and labor competition. Successfully maneuvering around competition is one of the biggest challenges in business and always has been.

Myth #2: The impact of technology is greater than ever.

False. Computer and information technology are only the biggest technologies *today*. Imagine dealing with the impact of the steam engine, the assembly line, mechanized factories, railroad shipping, and more. There will always be a "next" technology. Fifty years from now, our current cutting-edge technology will look quaint to that generation of businesspeople. They will imagine that their market is the most competitive ever ... but think of intergalactic competition and the robot labor force delivering virtual services and experiences ... YIKES!

It isn't technology and competition that are influencing our current lapse in developing soft skills in leadership. It's that the priorities and measurements being set by many current business leaders are quantitative. Many of these leaders are just more comfortable managing at a distance through the data. This is the antithesis of exceptional leadership because the process takes a leader's highly developed skill set and subjugates it to "the metrics." Why is this a problem? Because even the best technical leaders have trouble finding people's real upside in the numbers. Even the most sophisticated trend analyst in the world will miss much of what a learning leader can discern by paying the right kind of attention to people.

We have to admit that today's technical tools and access to good measurements have made being a competent leader easier. You just can't go all in with "managing by numbers." It can be perilous for any organization that can't see that it's happening or break away from it. The root problem is using numbers alone to make decisions, attempting to use data to get to know people, or trying to inspire people with numbers. Overuse of quantification can cause a leader to confuse targets with purpose. There are things that numbers can do and things that numbers can't do. Knowing which is which will be one of the key attributes of today's successful leaders.

Being an exceptional leader means being unafraid to consider and weigh the subjective and the non-quantitative things like:

- Morale
- Commitment
- Support
- Inspiration
- Buy-in
- Confusion
- Timing
- Momentum
- Lethargy
- Boldness
- Saturation
- Will
- Enthusiasm

- Potential
- Cooperation
- Openness

Leadership Myopia

The main danger of being a quant-jock (a term I have heard used to describe numbers and data-manipulation wizards) is succumbing to myopia. Business myopia is a problem with a leader's vision. Myopic leaders may see things that are up close (short-term) with perfect clarity, but have a lot of trouble with their distance (long-term) vision. This is a real liability because it affects the ability to do the one thing that only a leader can do for a business—inspire.

When you think about and see only things that are up close, you lose the ability to scan the horizon. You become uncomfortable talking about things like purpose, vision, and destiny. Those concepts just don't show up in the next quarter, which is as far as the myopic leader can see.

Leadership myopia also affects your rear view, keeping leaders from remembering the lessons found in their businesses' histories. This short view can become a critical handicap for a leader and can actually endanger a business or organization. What makes leadership myopia even more dangerous to businesses is that the affected leader is often the only one unaware of the problem.

I was fortunate to be a part of a small team asked to decide the long-term focus of a business that had been taken over by new ownership. The business was healthy, but adrift. There had been five changes in leadership in the previous eight years. At a branch level (where the real business was being done) there were competent, ambitious people doing good work. What had suffered was the company's collective identity. There was a lot of "good old days" nostalgia and no real sense of purpose or excitement about the future. The business was running on momentum alone, and the numbers reflected that fact.

The meeting included a few very-tenured company field executives along with the new leaders installed by the new ownership. It was a very good team of smart people with the best of intentions. The long-term employees were very passionate about what this company could become. This was the very reason why they had stuck it out through all of the volatility. They really believed the company could be great and important. The new imported leaders got caught up in the passion, and together they agreed on a bold new purpose for the business: This company would leverage its entrepreneurial culture and street-level horsepower to become the acknowledged leader in its industry. It already had the product, the footprint, and talent (which are usually the hard parts), and needed only a good long-term plan and inspired leadership to begin the climb towards its destined position—a dominant brand. So far, so good, right?

Everybody flew home filled with excitement and anticipation. "We're finally going to kick this organization into high gear," the veterans said to their teams. "The good old days are still ahead of us."

A few weeks passed. The new executives appropriately busied themselves meeting people and getting to know the organization. They necessarily met with accountants and controllers, learning their way around the numbers. The time came to begin to communicate the vision to the broader team.

A whole company call was set up with a web presentation set to go real-time with everyone. The call got off to a great start with business plans and goals shared with the whole team. The call was to finish with the sharing of the company's visions for the future. Here is what it had become: "The Company is an industry leader and demonstrates an annual growth rate of 10%+ while delivering earnings of greater than 15% over the next fiscal year."

It happened. Myopia had set in and ruined a fantastic opportunity to lead and inspire. When questioned by the company veterans about what had happened to the inspiring statement of purpose they had all crafted together, the executives said all of the predictable things. "It needs to be measurable. We must be accountable to earnings at a branch level." They had lost sight of the horizon. They had in those few weeks convinced themselves that everyone would be inspired by the numbers that had inspired them.

By emphasizing the numerical targets, the new "vision" satisfied the suits and lost the real producers. Leadership myopia begins by affecting the vision of the leader. It quickly spreads to affect the leader's vocabulary. The big words are the first to go. Passion, destiny, purpose, love, greatness, mission, dominance. The words that move people are obscured and fall into disuse. After a time, a myopic leader will actually become embarrassed and self-conscious when these words are used.

A good metaphor for leadership vision is a rudder on a ship. The longer and deeper the rudder, the straighter the boat will travel towards its destination. A short rudder will make any watercraft susceptible to small waves and crosscurrents. It will be very hard to steer and keep on course, taking much longer to reach its destination if it gets there at all. The vision analogy is obvious and accurate. An exceptional leader needs bifocals; he needs to be able to focus clearly on both short- and long-term targets. He needs to be able to set up quantitative goals to measure progress against interim benchmarks.

Being a bifocal leader means understanding how an inspiring picture of the future keeps people working hard and working happy in the present. A clear vision of the future is one that anyone in your organization can understand how he or she fits in to. The back-office staff, the executives, the accountants, the sellers, the servicers, everyone.

An inspired vision of "what we can become" can actually pull people in, multiply their effectiveness, and propel them forward. This kind of shared vision actually takes on a motivating force of its own. It's a leader's responsibility to boldly articulate where everyone is going and how we're going to get there. When leaders know how to embrace and articulate the focus of the business, they create energy and belief that can carry an organization to heights that simply could not be reached in any other way.

☑WELKnote:

Do not let the influence of data and consensus-building shrink the importance of communicating and inspiring your team. People want purpose and passion.

Chapter 7 - Leadership Personality Archetypes

We have explored many crucial ideas for leaders who aspire to improve themselves and, by extension, their results. Let's revisit two of those ideas as a way to introduce leadership personality archetypes:

#1 – **With study and consistent attention, leaders can develop powerful influence over people and processes.** This influence will directly affect the results of their teams.

#2 – **Reputation begins with a decision.** Your personal and professional reputation is not something that is assigned to you or something that happens accidentally: It's something you earn. Once earned, a reputation can be very hard to change. You can affect it by something you do or don't do, by something that is or is not true, by something that is said by one of your peers to another, by a single act or by a series of actions. Being a leader means you're continually being evaluated by others. Once established, your reputation is there before you show up and it will be there after you go. Reputation is an amazingly powerful force in your life.

Wherever you work, regardless of industry, location, or the size of your organization, you can find the basic leadership personality archetypes. These are the styles, postures, and characteristics that make up the overall population of leaders everywhere. Like most types, it can seem that there are many more than there actually are. We can be distracted by how leaders want to be seen and how they actually are perceived. The best way to understand leadership personality archetypes is to see them as specific combinations of those two factors cited above: influence and reputation.

The study of leadership types is worthwhile and valuable because it helps us understand how we are perceived and help us to make changes if we decide we should. Unlike your temperament, your personality archetype is made up of decisions, not predispositions. A leadership archetype contains six main variables. How you're perceived as a leader can be understood as a unique combination of these factors. Leadership archetypes are constructed around leaders who have similar weights and strengths in the six factors, but every leader is original and unique in some key ways.

Ambition

Credibility

Competence

Expressiveness

Sensitivity

Self-Awareness

Think of these six factors as the "recipe" for your leadership personality. Someone who wanted to make another "You" would have to sprinkle in different amounts of the ingredients above. As mentioned above, these factors are not your native temperament; they are the pieces that come together to form your leadership personality. You can remember the six factors with the acrostic A.C.C.E.S.S.

Ambition

Ambition sometimes gets a bad rap. People are often described as being too ambitious, and it can lead to distrust. That is not a true or fair understanding of ambition. Ambition is *fuel*, and it's as simple as that. Does a leader have enough ambitious fuel to do the things that need to be done? Does the leader have enough ambition to learn new things so he can improve his performance?

Ambition makes people go. It's an extension of a person's self-esteem and answers the question, "What does this leader expect from himself or herself?" Think for a moment on these questions:

What is your level of ambition?

Do you consider it a strength?

Does it fuel you?

Would people describe you as ambitious?

Do you like being called ambitious?

Do you consider it a compliment?

Credibility

This word seems to be misused a lot in business. Credibility is not how well you do your job or know your stuff; that's Competence. Credibility is how well people *think* you know your stuff. Credibility is built on perception and reputation, while competence is built on actual ability. How would you score yourself on credibility? Are you seen as an expert? Do your ideas influence decisions? Some leaders actually perceive that they have more credibility than they deserve. How would you rate your overall level of credibility in the eyes of the people you care about?

Competence

This is straight-up know how. Someone's level of competence is exactly equal to her ability to know or do a certain thing. Competence is a fascinating concept because we are all highly competent in some areas and completely incompetent in others.

We are all constructed with a particular mix of competence levels in every area of our life. This gives us an objective sensitivity to people who don't know how to do things. It also allows us to recognize false competence almost immediately.

You can fake credibility, but you can't fake competence. How would you rate your competence in the important areas of your job as a leader?

Expressiveness

Many leaders are drastically under-developed in this area. They are competent leaders, and they know what needs to be happening with the people on their teams, but they just don't know the most effective ways to get their messages across. Because of this, whatever level of competence they have achieved is blunted and muted. Expressiveness covers a number of bases. It includes communication skills (verbal and written), body language, and leadership vocabulary.

For some leaders, very specific kinds of expressiveness become crucially important to their success. This could be conference call skills, public speaking skills, webinar expressiveness, or boardroom communication skills.

I worked at a company where nearly every important decision was made on conference calls with different groups of people on each one. What if you were a highly skilled and highly ambitious person working at the company, but you were just no good at conference calls? Maybe you had a weak voice, you interrupted a lot, or you had a poor vocabulary. What if you were an extrovert and developed a reputation for just blurting ideas out on calls without the necessary forethought? What if you were an introvert and people thought that you were not confident or opinionated? This would severely detract from your ability to impact important business decisions, maybe for your whole career. This could explain a lack of career momentum for a person who was completely unaware of this deficit in her overall leadership persona.

Whatever kind of expressiveness is important in your leadership role, you must master it to be able to optimize the other five parts of your leadership personality. How would you rate yourself on expressiveness?

Sensitivity

This may be the least learnable of the six parts of a leader's personality. Sensitivity is the leader's ability to feel what is happening with a person or a group. The most effective leaders can sense the energy in people and know when it's the right time to say and do certain things. Sometimes it's time sympathy, sometimes it can be the moment for an empathetic response, but most of the time it's just having a sense of good timing.

Sensitivity to others' temperaments is also crucial to a leader's success, so much so that we will tackle that big topic in a dedicated section of the book.

We have all experienced the cringe that comes when a leader says the wrong thing (competence) at the wrong time (sensitivity) in the wrong way (expressiveness). We have all seen a leader "lose the room" with an insensitive remark or a topic that is not suited to the audience. The main problem with the insensitive leader is that he almost always thinks that the problem is the audience. It's a classic "they don't know what they don't know" scenario.

Self-Awareness

Nothing will neuter a leader's overall effectiveness faster than a lack of self-awareness. This particular part of the leader's personality changes more over time than any other of the six parts. Most of us probably start our careers with too much self-awareness. We ponder how we look, how we sound, how we are being perceived. As a young leader, I probably thought more about these things than I did about the actual coaching and leading I was doing. It's possible to think about perception more than content, and some of us are guilty of it. Usually this is just a temporary development stage for new leaders.

What often happens with leaders is just the opposite of that. As they succeed in their roles and rise in their companies, their self-awareness continues to recede. Leaders can convince themselves that their ideas are best and that the care they once took in their communications and relationships does not matter as much now that they're the big boss. It's almost a business cliché: the President or CEO with little or no self-awareness. It can get to the point where they can no longer learn and no longer be coached.

This is how the "Peter Principle" plays out even at the top of many companies. The ego-driven leaders, who were once very good at accepting coaching and other people's ideas, become autocrats. The absolute lack of self-awareness often keeps them from understanding that they're not leading effectively. Leaders with that level of self-awareness don't buy a lot of books on leadership because they already believe they know everything.

As we discussed in another chapter, the bottom line is all learning leaders need to maintain their humility actively. Amazingly, the personality trait of humility and a healthy level of self-awareness will make you the most effective leader you can be. You will see what people need and what they expect, and you will know exactly how you can get better. How do you feel about your level of self-awareness? Do you think this is an area that could use some attention?

These are the six pieces of the leadership personality puzzle. How they come together forms your leadership archetype. Every one of us is original and unique based on the strong and weak parts of our personality. The great news is that all six of these variables can be strongly influenced. The key to influencing these traits is understanding that you can improve. Believing that you're not a finished product and that you have a lot of upside as a leader *because* of these existing areas of improvement is called *humility*, and that's your most powerful trait as a leader.

☑WELKnote:

It can be hard to maintain a healthy level of self-awareness as a leader, especially as you move higher in your organization.

Exceptional Leaders Are Active Learners

Chapter 8 - Building a Better You

You are as good as you know how to be. That is true for all of us, and it is always true.

The most powerful thing you can do to improve as a leader is to work directly on your own leadership skill set. It is not working on the people on your team, not setting goals and targets, not prioritizing and optimizing ... it is working on yourself as a person and a leader.

Most of the prevailing ideas we all have about management and leadership are rooted in the one overriding concept that good managers and leaders are effective because they know how to get people to do the things for the company, division, department, or district to succeed. When we begin to call ourselves "managers" or "leaders," we should automatically begin to define ourselves by the impact we have on others.

It's certainly true that a manager who can effectively organize and measure people's efforts and activities will be seen as a successful manager. Because of this truth, the impact of "working on yourself" is often lost or under-emphasized. Most of the current information and training on management miss this most powerful and reliable way to improve your results. The idea of working on yourself as a *growth strategy* is not often discussed.

Working on yourself means purposely doing and learning things that will make you a better leader/manager/person. Most of the really classic business literature is intensely focused on this idea, but sadly, self-improvement has left the business section of the bookstore and re-rooted itself in the pop psychology aisle.

Why has this shift happened? As managers, we simply prefer to think that big improvements will come from other people changing rather than thinking that we can (and should) grow ourselves to earn these business gains. Another reason may be that we forget that we are the constants in our business. There's going to be considerable change and churn in most of today's organizations.

When you're managing in the white water, you'll usually do best by managing the constants, starting with yourself. A valuable core belief would be to expect bigger outcomes, bigger opportunities, bigger leverage points, and bigger possibilities if we focus on becoming bigger people. Over time, we can actually increase the *capacity* to lead. Capacity is not changed easily, but when capacity increases, a leader has every right to expect more success for himself and his team.

☑WELKnote:

Purposeful self-improvement is the cornerstone of exceptional leadership.

Chapter 9 - Why Leaders Get Stuck

You've been at your job for a few years or more. You know the job and what is expected of you. You know your employees, what makes them tick, what ticks them off, how to get the most out of them, and what they will do in each situation. You also know the shareholders, the mission statement, the forecasts, the risks, and the rewards.

In short, you've found your rhythm.

Then it happens. Gradually things start to change, not enough to make you do anything differently, just enough to make you loosen your collar a bit. There are new employees, new policies, new products, maybe a new board member or two. Change is all around you. You don't even remember the moment it happened. This slackening does not happen all at once. It was a deleted email here and there, a missed meeting or two, a casual comment that you let go. It was a million things that added up to this. You got too comfortable and now something is wrong.

By *comfortable* we mean that you just started to care a little less about the details. You were more easily distracted. You were not as invested emotionally in the results. You felt confident and secure in your role. Frankly, you wanted to just coast for a bit. After all, you certainly earned it … or so you kept telling yourself.

And now you're being passed by. New opportunities aren't as plentiful. You used to be included in everything and everyone seemed to want your input, but now for some reason your opinion doesn't seem to hold the same value.

If you had been paying attention, you would have seen this coming. When was the last time you actually got up before the alarm because you were so excited to get to work? When was the last time you read a self-improvement book? Attended a workshop? Learned a brand new skill? When was the last time you felt "inspired?"

The hardest part about change is giving up your confidence. Learning something new could mean you aren't the authority for a short time. You won't be the "go to" person. When you continually try to improve, it's harder to keep up the pretense of "I've got this figured out" that so many great leaders seem to possess.

But do they really have it all figured out?

I remember the day I heard the comment, "The thing I love about this job is that you never really arrive." It was in middle of a professional "coasting" moment. I had a good year the year before, had hit all of my targets, and was feeling good about my contributions to our company. I don't remember who the speaker was; I just remember how I felt upon hearing that my "best" would now be expected of me and my team. Seriously? I had just knocked it out of the park, and you want me to do even better next year? Can't we just celebrate this amazing year for a while before you lay the hammer down? How unfair.

At the time, it seemed like a punch in the gut, but it would happen year after year. All businesses are striving for growth, and if you aren't growing (we've all heard this before), then you're dying.

So it's time to go back to work. Time for a gut check and an honest evaluation. A personal inventory is always important, but even more so if you feel you've plateaued. If we were to ask about your leadership, what would your team say? What would be in the very private survey they took?

Be fair to yourself. Not all reflection should be critical. Write BOTH lists. Where do you get high marks and where do you fall a bit short?

What are you going to do about the areas where you fall short? What are some growth opportunities you need to take advantage of? When will you start, and what will you do?

☑WELKnote:

Even experienced leaders can easily fall into a rut if they do not intentionally challenge themselves to grow.

Chapter 10 - Hacking into Your Own Life

We have all learned the word "hacking" from the IT world which describes a process of altering technology in a way the original developers did not intend. Hackers are not usually acting in the best interest of the owners. Some rogue hackers have achieved notoriety for their skills.

These days, we hear about "life hacks" from experts on the TED stage and blogs. These are very positive messages designed to help us look with fresh eyes on some of the small (a new way to tie your shoes) and large (how to have better personal relationships) opportunities we have to improve our lives.

What does this have to do with us as leaders? The idea of hacking is useful because it means that things can be altered to do what they would not have previously done. How can this simple, borrowed idea apply to your personal and professional lives?

Our lives and careers are powered mostly by momentum, inertia, and other external forces. We do our best professionally, and as leaders we understand that our work matters. We influence other people's lives, and we know it's serious business.

We have a lot in common because we are all driven by the same kinds of momentum and influenced by the same cultural and economic forces. Restated, we actually have a shocking amount in common.

What do we have in common?

- We are old enough that we can feel our age.

- We have accomplished some things and feel that we are successful.
- We consider ourselves to be smart.
- We have strongly-held opinions about politics, religion, and culture.
- Many of those opinions have never changed.
- Most of us have a few close friends.
- We have moved a few times, usually for work.
- Very few of us have any creative output of any kind outside of work.
- Most of us follow sports or popular culture.
- As leaders, we feel like we have good judgment and competence in our roles.
- Most of us think of ourselves as "high character" people.
- The things that anger us are mostly trivial (traffic, uncontrollable events, etc.).
- We are for the most part "happy," but would not use the word "joyful."
- We know what we like when it comes to books, music, movies, and TV.

The forces at work in our lives are homogenizing forces. These forces, when left alone, will make us all more alike over time. Becoming more alike takes no decisive action on our part, but becoming more individual absolutely does.

This is where the hacking part comes in.

There are deliberate thoughts and actions that we can introduce into our lives that counteract the forces of momentum. There are simple changes we can make that can alter our trajectories just one or two degrees. These one or two degrees, when multiplied by months and years, will change our overall directions and possibly even our destinations.

There are three high-impact areas for serious life hacking: routines, information, and aspiration. Sounds simple enough, right?

☑WELKnote:

Leaders sometimes need to make deliberate changes in the way they do things.

Chapter 11 - Leveraging Routines

Routines are an amazingly powerful part of our personal and professional lives. If you take anything, even a small thing, and multiply it by 1,000 or 10,000, it becomes very big. Routines are the area of your life that can help or hurt you the most. If you understand the importance of routines in your life, you also understand the need to leverage and manage them to be the person and the leader you want to be. So how do you analyze your routines?

List the things you do every single day. Mentally go through your day and list everything that is built into your daily activity. Don't list "go to work," as that's not a routine; that's your job. But if you stop at Starbucks every day on the way to work, that's a routine. Most people have a dozen or so routines they duplicate every day, with some significant disparity between weekdays and weekends. If that's true for you, it might be worthwhile to make two lists, one for weekdays and one for weekends.

Once you have your list (or lists), you can do some investigation and discovery about yourself. First, you'll want to look at your list and see if there's any routine that will represent risk or danger to you if you continue it. Habits and routines are fascinating because they can form so quickly and be so hard to stop once they're knit into your life. This is exactly why they're worth studying. Here are some questions to help you in this process:

- Do you have any routines that you already know you will not be able to continue indefinitely?

- Do you have a routine that adds energy to your life?
- Do you have a routine that comes between you and someone you love?
- Do you have any routines that make you really proud?
- Is there a habit or routine that embarrasses you?
- Do you have a routine that does not really make any sense in your life any more?
- What is your best work or leadership routine?

Being objective about these kinds of questions and answers will put you in a rare category of individuals who are living the examined life, actively looking at how they live and how they might live better.

Now look into your life to discover where some great habits and routines could be, but are not:

- Do you have any routines that engage you intellectually?
- What routines do you have that challenge you physically?
- Is there something you see yourself doing, but don't actually do?
- Is there a habit or routine you could add to your life that could create more energy for you to use in other areas?
- Where in your life are you consistently creative?
- Is there a routine you could develop that would bring more interesting people into your life?

Habits and routines are a hyper-potent area of your life where you can gain or lose a lot. It's accurate to say that the majority of people's lives are simply the sum total of their routines. Those of us who are lucky enough to have many choices have to pay even closer attention to our routines because more of our schedule is in our own control. As leaders, understanding our routines and habits is crucial for us to be able to lead people towards improvement and higher potential.

In a sense, *we are what we choose to do and choose not to do.* High performers and leaders need to audit their routines every once in a while to make sure their hands are on the steering wheel, taking their lives exactly where they want them to go.

☑WELKnote:

Routines and habits are two of the most powerful forces in your life. Leverage them to create the outcomes you want.

Chapter 12 - Your Personal Board of Directors

This is a very powerful idea borrowed from corporate America. It's something that almost all exceptional leaders have in common, whether they formalize the idea or not: the board of directors. Everyone knows what a board of directors is. Most growth-oriented companies and start-ups organize a group of people with various talents and skill sets to help set the direction for the organization. Typically, the members are chosen for the positive impact they can have on the organization's decisions and strategies.

Have you ever seen a BOD (board of directors) list for a start-up company and been blown away by the diversity and power of the group? I have. I reviewed a prospectus for a start-up just a few days ago. On page three was the list of names for the BOD, and I was floored at the combined power and experience of the group. The immediate thought was that this group of dynamic leaders working together could and would do extraordinary things. I immediately bought some stock, as you might have guessed.

So how do we apply the idea of the BOD to our personal development as leaders?

We can leverage the power of the BOD to make sure we are constantly improving our leadership skill sets and our awareness of areas where we can improve. Norman Vincent Peale was the first to write about the power of this idea. He famously called it "The Mastermind Group" and wrote at length about using our relationships and our imaginations to drive purposeful self-improvement. He understood, as did his mentor Andrew

Carnegie, the power of deliberate time being spent with people who can influence you for the better.

As exceptional leaders, we're going to be growing, learning, and changing throughout our careers. We shouldn't leave anything to chance or rely on the "accidental influencers" we bump into. Being open to and deliberately in search of the right influencers will be a big part of reaching our potential as leaders.

So how do you start organizing your BOD?

1. Start by thinking about people who have been positively influential for you in the past. Who are some of the people who have helped you have the success you have experienced so far?

2. Keep your perspective open wide, as these influencers will not just be people you worked with. Some of your most powerful influencers will be teachers, coaches, friends, authors, speakers, and peers.

3. Think about yourself as a leader right now. Think about the leader you would like to be. Consider some of the leaders that you know who have some of the attributes you aspire to.

We've been helping people think through their BOD's for decades, and the most common block is thinking too small and finite with the BOD concept. Your leadership skills set and persona can be influenced by ANYONE. The BOD is a personal construction designed to do one thing: help you develop into the leader you want to be. Drawing from more sources from more different places is a good thing. Your personal BOD is an "internal organization." It exists just for you and it will change as you move through your career. Here is a list of some of the people I have considered "Board Members" through my career. These people had a powerful influence on me and absolutely helped me develop into the leader I am today:

Chuck Reddick – The first real leader and mentor I ever worked with. He taught me about self-improvement and the power of communication.

We worked together for almost 20 years and still speak often today. He was my original mentor and absolutely influential in helping me understand my strengths as a leader.

Earl Nightingale – Author and speaker. Famous for his "Strangest Secret" recording in the 1950s. His message and delivery had a powerful impact on me even though I never met him.

Muhammad Ali – Boxer and humanitarian. Ali's combination of principles, performance, and dynamism had a big impact on me and still does. I got to shake his hand once and thanked him for being who he is.

Jim Rohn – Author and speaker. Mr. Rohn had a level of humanity that I had never seen in a leadership and self-improvement trainer before. His simple wisdom was a powerful influence on the way I used communication as a leader. I talked to him briefly once at one of his seminars. He was as gracious as I expected him to be.

George M. – This guy was a walking nightmare of a leader. Arrogant, self-centered, and absolutely ineffective. Why is he on my BOD? He was an "anti role-model" for me during my formational years when I was a young leader. Watching how he affected people and how little influence he actually had (even though he was the president of a big company) really helped me understand the responsibility and privilege of leadership.

Tom Peters – Management consultant, author, and speaker. I met Mr. Peters only once briefly, but he had an important role in my development. He was so passionate about what leaders and companies could do, the roles they could play in our lives, and the importance of attacking the status quo. Through his many books, he affected my attitude and outlook as a leader.

Interesting list, right? I actually worked with only two of the six people listed above, but the others had the same kind of strong and permanent influence on me as a developing leader. I am pretty sure that none of the people listed above ever knew they were a part of my personal BOD, and none of the people above are on my current BOD. Not because they're no longer important, but because I have other things to learn now, and I need different people and different ideas to teach and influence me.

I'm not going to share my current BOD. It's personal, remember?

Here are the six steps for putting your BOD together:

1. **Do a little thinking about yourself and your current leadership performance.** Ask yourself some questions: What is working for me? What is not? Who is influencing me now? When do I have the most fun in my leadership role? What have I been doing the same way for too long? What are my greatest leadership assets? Most important: Can I describe the next version of me as the leader I would like to become?

2. **Think about some people who have some of the spirit, capability, attitude, enthusiasm, credibility, and influence that you would like to have.** They can be other leaders, peers, friends, authors, speakers, bloggers, poets, musicians, celebrities, athletes … whoever. They can be dead or alive. They can be people you know or people you don't. Make a list of these people.

3. **Review this list and think about what you would like to learn or assimilate from each person.** Who on your list do you have access to? How will you access him? It can be in-person, over the phone, by reading his books, by seeing his work.

4. **For the people you have personal access to, ask yourself a few more questions.** Will this person give me some of his or her time? Will this person give me unfiltered opinions? Can I do something in return? It's not necessary to tell people that they're going to be on your BOD unless you think it will help the relationship.

5. **Post your BOD somewhere you can see it and make a commitment to seek out input, content, lessons, and conversations in any form you can get it from the members of your board.**

6. **Review the concept occasionally and ask yourself if it's adding any value to your development as a leader.** You may need to be more active and overt, or you may need to shake up your BOD.

Why should corporations and start-ups be the only ones benefitting from an influential Board of Directors? Get your BOD organized as soon as you can think about how your board members may be able to influence your development as a leader. It's a powerful idea, and once you see the impact of it, you can share it with some of the people you're responsible to. I'll bet that you'll end up on a few boards of directors!

☑**WELKnote:**

High-performance leaders have advisors and mentors. They learn to aggregate and leverage the best advice and the best examples they can find.

Chapter 13 - The Power of Aspiration

Along with routines and ideas, the power of aspiration is one of the most potent life-changing forces. For most leaders, aspiration has been the fuel that has gotten them to where they are in life. They aspired to a certain lifestyle, a professional career, an income level, or fitness level. Their aspirations drove them to do the things they needed to do to create the life situation they wanted.

The opposite is also true; areas in our lives where we had no particular aspirations did not get the same attention or effort. Many successful people have regrets associated with a lack of aspiration in a certain area like health, education, or relationships. We all make these choices, and aspiration (or the lack of aspiration) is what drives the outcomes.

It's possible to forget the power of aspiration for periods of time, especially as you age. We have all met people who forgot about the potency of aspiration, but aspiration is so important that it can explain nearly everything in your life. Your life and your accomplishments can be understood simply by thinking about what you *did* and *did not* aspire to in all of these areas.

> "*You cannot escape the results of your thoughts. Whatever your present environment may be, you will fall, remain, or rise with your thoughts. You will become as small as your controlling desire; as great as your dominant aspiration.*"
>
> –James Allen

Lives are shaped by aspirations everywhere you look. Even seemingly inexplicable choices can be easily understood when the aspirations are known. Leaders who understand this are never mystified by other people's choices. When you take the time to try to understand people's motives and aspirations, you become a person who can connect with others in a unique and authentic way. This ability can make you a fantastic parent, spouse, parent, friend, business partner, or leader.

Getting to Know People You Have Known for Years

Enlightened leaders understand that they do not always get to see the "real" people they lead. Often, the folks we work with act in the way they think they're supposed to act at work. They say the things they're supposed to say, agree with things they're supposed to agree with, and show you (the leader) the parts of themselves that they believe to be the most attractive and competent. This is one of the reasons why understanding the aspirations of your team members is not easy ... you're not seeing the real people most of the time.

Many leaders do not even care really to know the people on their teams. This is their choice, and it's one way to lead. Most of us have worked with this kind of boss. But this experience presents a real opportunity for you as a leader, an opportunity to enhance your people's experience at work, and an opportunity for you to understand what really drives them. A leader who makes an effort really to *know* the people he or she leads can be quite a positive surprise for people.

The leader who takes the time to understand the aspirations of his team members has the opportunity to put them in situations and positions where they will perform best. This means that the overall team has a higher performance, along with other less tangible outcomes like work satisfaction, loyalty, and morale.

Here are a few recommended questions that can help a leader begin to understand the motives and aspirations of people on their team:

- What is your favorite part about your job? Your least favorite?
- What is something you're really good at that you do not get to do in your current role?
- What are the work accomplishments you're most proud of?
- What would make it more fun to come to work?
- Can you tell me about some of your career goals?
- What is the task you do regularly that often feels like a waste of time?
- What would you change about your job if you could?

Those questions would help any leader really begin to understand someone on the team. Most leaders would be amazed at how much better they would know this person after this twenty-minute conversation.

Look at just one of the questions above: "What are the work accomplishments you're most proud of?"

A leader can learn much from just this one simple question. When asked this question, people often clarify "work accomplishments," which tells a leader that most of what they're really proud of falls outside of work. If the person talks about longevity, you know he's motivated by stability. If the person talks about an award, she's motivated by recognition. If the person talks about a comparative measure, she's motivated by competition. If a person talks about an idea or initiative that they were was responsible for, he aspires to be seen as smart or creative.

Of course, people are complicated and can be motivated by many different things. Engaging in these kinds of conversations can give a leader at least a base-line understanding of their people. Asking these conversations will clearly identify you as the kind of leader who is willing to try to understand who your people are and why they come to work.

☑WELKnote:

Aspiration and ambition can provide the fuel you will need to accomplish your objectives as a leader.

Chapter 14 - Using New Ideas to Optimize Your Life

Being high-performance people means we must be willing to examine our own lives objectively. This kind of examination and discovery must be deliberate. It does not come naturally. Most people are so weighed down with reactions, routines, opinions, and prejudices that they end up making few actual choices about their lives on a day-to-day basis. They are on a treadmill of their own making, set to a certain speed and direction. This unconscious treadmill, not their personal and deliberate choices, dictates the way they spend their days, weeks, months, and years.

Many people will never seek out ideas that can improve their situations, especially if it contradicts or makes them question the way they may be doing things. Thinking competitively, this fact makes it much easier to succeed over a long career. As time goes on there are fewer and fewer people actually trying to improve themselves. Think about the personal power you can accrue by gaining experience over time *and* working purposefully to improve yourself.

Life Experience + Active Learning = Unbeatable Combination

So where do you go to actively improve yourself? Where are the ideas you need in order to optimize your life? That depends on what you're trying to do. John Wooden, the oft-quoted former UCLA basketball coach, said, "Five years from now, you're the same person you are now, except for the people you've met and the books you've read." This is absolutely true, and you could probably add experiences to the list as well. We can agree that in five, ten, or twenty years you'll be the same person you are today unless you're influenced by events, information, and people.

Here is where you'll find a critical difference between high-performance people and everyone else: The high-performance person *chooses* what he will be influenced by. Everyone else treats these life-defining influences as a part of their environment, as something that is happening to them without their choice or consent.

Your challenge as a learning leader is to find lots of ways to get new ideas into your life. Professional relationships have changed over the last few years. Many of us are now working across several groups on distinct projects, instead of working with just one group in an ongoing workflow. Today we may find ourselves with 400 "connections," but having no real conversations. We all need at least a few people in our lives, outside of our own families, with whom we can have the big conversations. We need to be having conversations about the purpose of our work, about lifestyles, about leveraging our jobs to learn new skills, about aspiration and ambition.

These are the big-picture conversations that introduce new thoughts and often cause us to change our approaches to what we're doing. As Eleanor Roosevelt said, "Great minds discuss ideas; average minds discuss events; small minds discuss people." This explains why most of us will only have a few people in our lives with whom we can get into the big idea stuff, but dozens who would be happy to gossip with us all day.

Take a few minutes and make a list of the idea people you have in your life. These are the people with whom you could easily have a big-picture conversation. They may not always agree with you, but they can share this kind of dialog and get you thinking in new directions.

Most of us only have a precious few people in this category. Some of us don't have any. You need at least a few people helping you live an examined life. Thinking and talking consistently on the themes of purpose, direction, and philosophy can add many facets to your life. It's just like looking at your life and your work through a different lens—you see colors and contrasts you could not see on your own. Make it a priority to identify a few of these people and slowly build a dialog with them. They need it just as much as you do, and some of these connections will transcend their origins. They may start as relationships formed at work, church, or even the golf course, but end up being something much more.

Leveraging information and ideas is a crucial part of living a high-performance life. When we're influenced by new information and new ideas, we literally change our minds. We get the creative parts of our minds working to improve things and see old issues in new ways. Often these new thoughts manifest themselves as bigger expectations and bigger goals. As leaders, the potency of new ideas is multiplied. The leader benefits personally, and as a larger and more learned person, she can influence the team far more effectively.

☑WELKnote:

Keep yourself open to new ideas. Be ready and able to change your mind about things. Welcome people and ideas that challenge your point of view.

Chapter 15 - Time Management

How long has it been since you turned off your computer without any unread messages? How about the last time you did everything on your "to do" list? Getting it all done and being totally caught up is a thing of the past. Being totally accessible through technology means there's seldom a lull in the action. The next email you read will mean more things for you to do. The voice mail messages you listen to will hold another issue for you to handle.

The real question is not, "How can I get it all done?" The better question is, "What are the things I can put off and should, and what are the things I shouldn't?"

Think of it like this. There are a hundred things you should do each day. Your job is to figure out which are the four or five that you MUST do and which ones you can procrastinate on.

I've seen people fool themselves by over-organizing, calling more meetings than necessary, or reading the same emails over and over. I know those things can be important, but mostly they're just a way to rationalize not doing the hard stuff or the things that aren't fun.

If you were pressed for an answer, would you say you're more proactive or reactive? Meaning, do you spend time more time answering emails, returning phone calls, and attending meetings, or do you make the necessary time to be actually innovative and productive?

Is your email determining your priorities, or are you? For one week, don't leave your email program on all day. Turn off the "push" feature on your phone that alerts you with every single email. Read your emails only three times a day: once when you first get in, once after lunch, and once at the end of the day. Limit yourself to no more than two hours of total time. If the thought of this makes you nervous, build in a few extra hours here and there so you will at least attempt to minimize your availability.

What time do you get up in the morning? Do you wake up before the alarm well rested? My guess is only a small percentage can say "Yes" to this, but getting up one hour earlier each day can add up to two extra hours of productivity.

What are your non-negotiable tasks for the day? Try to begin each day with the four or five things you decide you *must* accomplish. It's not important that you have an amazing gift of discernment in the beginning since you'll get better and better over time. Once you accomplish those things, move on to the things that just waste your time.

Start right now. What ***should*** you be doing instead of what you are? What is one thing that you have been putting off, the thing that you just need to buckle down and do? How about a list of things that you want to do but haven't had the time? What do you need to do that will help you grow as a leader? What should you be doing that might make you smarter or happier? Are you building in any time for your health? Are you spending enough time with the people you love?

These questions start you thinking about your schedule instead of just grinding it out day after day. Figure out how to manage your schedule instead of it managing you!

☑WELKnote:

The ability to manage your priorities and energy within the constraints of time is a master skill of success. Audit how you're spending your time and energy assets.

Chapter 16 - Your Professional Improvement Mandate

One of the hardest parts of leadership is managing self-limiting beliefs. It's not what you do that matters, but who you become in the process. It doesn't matter what company you work for, what job you do, if you're a stay-at-home mom or dad, or even if you're in between opportunities. Making the most out of every day is the ultimate euphoric feeling: that feeling that you left it all on the field, that the days fly by, that you're so busy you forget to eat, the idea that you could not possibly squeeze one more experience in and you're left feeling spent and unbelievably satisfied.

You don't know that feeling? Why not?

How can you be trusted to help cultivate other people's potential when you aren't living up to your own? It's one of the biggest reasons people ultimately fail at developing other people, which is the primary function of leadership. Most have heard the phrase "fake it 'til you make it," and many are living that out. It's okay to fake it for a while, provided you're doing the work that will get you where you want to go. This will require deep introspection and self-awareness. Leaders understand that the passage of time will either promote them or expose them, and they themselves will create the outcome ... whatever it turns out to be.

How can you be an amazing leader if you don't feel deserving of success? I can't tell you how many incredibly talented people I've met that have no idea how special they are. How does that happen? Was it something their parents said? An off-handed comment by a Grandparent? A parent of their best friend? A teacher that embarrassed them during class? A coach pushing too hard? A spouse (or ex-spouse)? A sibling? How can someone give all of his power to someone who is probably not living up to his own potential?

People spend millions of dollars on books, seminars, psychologists, and life coaches, trying to "live up to their potential." Just the fact that you want to up your personal game is a huge part of the battle. Making the decision to improve yourself in any area certainly is admirable. Have you ever met or spent time with someone who has made a commitment to grow or improve her life? Don't you love spending time with them? Have you ever *been* that person? The one others sought out? Maybe you were on the right path, you had it figured out, and then one day the spark was gone. The energy that made you jump out of bed had somehow disappeared.

Perhaps someone you value threw a big bucket of water on the "fire" that was fueling you. Maybe you just jumped in a big pool and extinguished yourself by not continuing to grow. Over time, you started to buy into what you believed were flaws about yourself. You accepted them as the truth.

I work with a great many business owners, and I ask them a few simple questions to understand what kind of internal dialog they might be experiencing. Here are the first few questions I start with:

- What would you like to get from our time together?
- Why do you think you need to improve?
- What do you think is holding your business back?
- What do you think is holding YOU back?
- Are you aware of any self-limiting beliefs?
- What is the worst thing someone has ever said about you?
- Is what they said true?

It would take days to answer these simple questions. Most people have never thought about their own self-limiting beliefs, the deep-down feelings of self-worth. After a lot of introspection, most people do come to the conclusion that what they were unconsciously believing isn't even true.

I love the title of Byron Katie's book *Who Would You Be Without Your Story?* You don't even have to read the book (but you should) to understand the point. What is your success story? What do you believe deep down in your gut you truly deserve? It's important to know because it will define you at some point. It will drive you or sabotage you, and it's totally your choice.

Leading people effectively requires an in-depth understanding of your own self-limiting beliefs and a huge dose of personal awareness, neither of which is easy to ascertain.

Let this be the time that you finally do something about the old tapes playing in your head that have been holding you back. There are people depending on you, even if it's only yourself.

☑WELKnote:

Consistent self-improvement is a must for a today's progressive leaders.

Chapter 17 - Toxic Beliefs for Leaders

We have studied hundreds of businesses over the years, and it's clear that most organizations excel to the degree their leaders believe in the talent, possibilities, and potential of their people. That sounds like a hopeful platitude that you might find on a motivational poster somewhere, doesn't it? Just give it some thought: "Organizations excel to the degree their leaders believe in the talent, possibilities, and potential of their people."

Now apply this idea to some of the businesses that you're most familiar with. Once you've had time to consider it, you'll think of examples of this kind of belief and situations where it was clearly missing. You'll realize that the statement is indisputably true.

Organizations that allow and promote a diversity of opinion, accept mannerly disputes, acknowledge excellence wherever it's found (from the mailroom to the boardroom), and share information liberally generally have a higher level of person-for-person productivity than more bureaucratic organizations. The worst offenders of this theory are companies where upper management consistently underestimates their own people's talent and capabilities. We've had an opportunity to work with many different organizations, representing several different industries, and it's been surprising to see how pervasive some of this thinking is.

There are quantitative metrics available showing comparative per-person revenue in organizations. You can imagine the disparity between the firms where people are allowed and expected to grow in responsibility while being challenged to improve and those organizations where people are kept in categories and classifications that management has pre-determined. What is really surprising is that the organizations that are most in need of new talent and new ideas are often the ones who are most guilty of "pigeon-holing" their own people.

Another shocking and dangerous problem we see again and again is organizations who believe their organizational chart is also their intelligence and talent chart. That is to say, they really believe that the distribution of titles in their business is an accurate reflection of talent, intellect, and creativity.

We refer to these kinds of growth-crushing ideas as "toxic beliefs." These are concepts, thought-patterns and ideas that, when adopted and absorbed at an executive level, can wound or even kill an organization from the inside out.

Here are some toxic beliefs that exist in many business organizations today. This list could be re-labeled "a recipe for obsolescence":

- People will do as little work as they possibly can.
- The status quo represents the least risk for our organization.
- Good ideas start at the top.
- We can cost-cut our way to growth.
- Full disclosure is not an option.
- The word *diversity* applies only to race and gender.
- Our organizational chart mirrors our people's intellectual level.
- Our executives do not need to work on their skill sets.
- We talk like a democracy, but act like a dictatorship.
- The clients won't leave because we are too good at what we do.

Think about your company. Are you practicing any toxic beliefs? Can you see where these ideas have stunted your growth or created unnecessary risk for your business or team?

Many of these toxic beliefs are legacy ideas that have been passed through organizations organically. Often they're so present and so pervasive that they're hard to see. These debilitating ideas can influence expectations and results for decades in some organizations. When you work in a broadly distributed organization with autonomous branches or divisions, you can really see how these kinds of beliefs can influence results. One branch has certain beliefs about what works, and the results over time will reflect those beliefs. Another division has its own biases that dictate their work and expectations. A skilled leader can learn to see and discern how false biases and toxic beliefs are showing up in the results. Once they're identified, they can be explained and addressed.

A leader should always expect push-back and skepticism when talking about organizational biases. People honestly do not believe that they're being influenced by, or that they are themselves promulgating, a toxic belief. It takes patience and a non-judgmental approach by the leader.

Everything starts with a progressive dialog with your team:

1. Identify a clear bias or errant supposition.

2. Explain how such a belief might have come into existence.

3. Talk through how this bias or belief is showing up in the results.

4. Ask for leaders on the team to personally take actions to prove that the bias or belief in question is wrong.

5. As results begin to accumulate, be prepared to provide additional training and/or support to help your team leaders succeed.

6. Once there are clear and demonstrable results that show the bias as false, share with the team and recognize your leaders for their successful work.

A leader who can learn to see and reverse negative beliefs on a team is a very valuable person. You will see leaders with these skills placed at the head of team after team. Often, these talented leaders end up being labeled as "turnaround specialists," but they are actually investigators and optimists. They can see where a negative organizational belief is hurting results, and they know how to act on it.

☑WELKnote:

You become what you think about. Are your thoughts helping or hurting you as a leader?

Exceptional Leaders Know That Coaching is Leadership in Action

Chapter 18 - How Developed Leaders Improve Their Teams

I have been both a student of leadership and an active business leader for over 20 years now. In that time, I've been able to work and consult with hundreds of business and organizational leaders. I have probably read over 500 books on business, management, success, coaching, personal development, and leadership. Add to that all of the seminars, articles, webinars, blogs, and workshops, and you have a person who has made a real effort over a span of many years to learn as much as I possibly could about leadership. I know that I'm not alone in this endeavor to identify what really works for leaders and to understand what the truly exceptional leaders know.

I'm saying all of this to introduce you to what has been the biggest surprise and disappointment in my career as a business leader and a student of business leaders. First, consider the overall volume and value of all the collective information that has been presented to us by the likes of Peters, Covey, Maxwell, Drucker, DePree, Rohn, Bennis, Collins, Gerber, Gladwell, Deming, Nightingale, Blanchard, Johnson, Senge, and so many more. Fresh and progressive information about how to be an effective leader has been presented with amazing frequency for over sixty years. In their time, the writings of Edward Deming and Peter Drucker in their time were just as revolutionary as what Tom Peters and Bob Waterman gave us thirty years later, and the ideas shared by Michael Gerber and Jim Collins twenty years after that. And the concepts and ideas just keep coming.

Any person with a serious desire to be a successful leader has amazing and invaluable leadership content readily available to them in the pages of these books. So what is the disappointment I am referring to? I am talking about the decline in what being a leader actually means to many people these days. It's amazing how much of what is called "leadership" has been diluted into something else entirely. The truth is that a lot of what is called leadership today is actually just supervision, evaluation, administration, and manipulation.

Even with all of this progressive and valuable leadership and management content available, most of today's so-called leaders are just quantifying and supervising. They really aren't leading at all. You've worked for these people and you see what everyone else sees: *that most leaders never actually influence the performance of their teams.* Think about that for a moment. Most of these leaders are nice people; they have some valuable career experience; they know their business; they have a nice title; they may have a nice office; they probably have a good income … and they do not actually influence the performance of the people they're responsible for.

Of course there are myths at work here as well. Some pervasive leadership myths are to blame for many managers' misunderstanding of how one actually becomes a great leader. **Here is a short list of these myths:**

- Leaders are highly charismatic.
- Leaders get their credibility from their title.
- Experience is what makes leaders great.
- Highly productive leaders focus on what is quantifiable.
- Self-improvement is more important at the start of a career.
- Tough-minded leaders are autocrats.
- The people at the top of the Org Chart have the best ideas.

I've been guilty of believing all of the above myths and more. Some leadership myths, when really believed, will absolutely affect a leader's ability to improve and develop. We will explore more of these myths and "toxic beliefs" elsewhere in the book.

The most common definitions of leadership talk about leadership being "the act of leading a group towards a common goal." Webster or Wikipedia would tell you that leadership is a noun. In a way, it's the "leadership is a noun" idea that is at the root of the problem. Leaders who truly want to influence people and performance are *verb leaders*. They are the kinds of leaders who have learned how to move people effectively towards their personal objectives and the objectives of the whole organization. They have learned how to coach and influence people to become more. They understand that there are specific leadership strategies and actions that exceptional leaders know and use.

One of the most important things that exceptional leaders know is that leadership can be complicated. It's a study and a craft, and it does not come "naturally" to anyone. They also know that there are no accidentally great leaders or coaches. The great news for all of us is that there are incredibly vital and reliable strategies that any learning leader can understand and put into practice. This is what we will be working on together in the pages of this book.

Our job is to help you learn these strategies and drastically raise your potential and influence as a leader. We look forward to working with you to discover both your current strengths and your exciting upside as a developing leader.

☑WELKnote:

Leaders should be measured by their ability to influence performance and produce results.

Chapter 19 - Developing People

The ability to actually develop people over time is one of the most significant differences between leaders and managers. Managers have the mindset to do the best they can with the people they have, while leaders learn how to take the people they have and make them better. Most experienced leaders and coaches know that the best way to begin to influence people's perceptions of themselves is to affirm their talents and value gradually and very persistently. Most people are not used to another person looking at them and actually seeing more talent and more upside than everyone else perceives. This is exactly what exceptional leaders do.

Great coaches and leaders would much rather be guilty of overestimating a person's ability than underestimating it. The most effective leaders know and understand that once you peel back all of their formal leadership functions, they're in the "high expectations business." So how do we begin to turn these high expectations we have for our team members into real results?

It starts with a vision for each person having a bigger and more important role on your team. You have to take time to be with your people and explain how you see them expanding their roles and their impact in the organization as you work towards their (and your) vision. You must explain that you believe that they could be a much more influential part of the team, and get their thoughts and insights about the best ways to do this.

In the past, I have actually had to apologize to people on my team for not giving them enough responsibility and underutilizing their skills. The key here is to give everyone an important piece of the overall vision that they alone are responsible for. It must be tangible, measurable, and greater responsibility than they had before. If you can tie an incentive to an expected increase, then do it. An incentive tied to any kind of production increase is a no-risk proposition for you because you pay for such incentives out of the growth attained. Incentives should be organized with the full expectation that the goals will be realized or exceeded.

Often, the new responsibilities that you assign to people will be in areas that they themselves have recognized as areas of low performance. Be prepared to discover complete mismatches between people and their areas of highest interest. *Low* performance organizations match people with their preconceived competencies, to the stuff on their resume, or to what they studied in college many years ago. *High* performance organizations can hit warp speed by matching people with their areas of passion.

Here are a few examples. Susan types 100 words a minute, can take dictation, and is always coming up with crazy and workable marketing ideas. She's an original. Where can she make the most difference on your team? It's your job to find the best way to use her unique combination of talents to help the team. Jimmy is a "geek" who works in the IT department who also happens to be a fantastic public speaker. Maria works in fulfillment and has many years of experience with the company. She's also an excellent interviewer and has been deployed as a company value spokesperson.

Learning to discover and leverage talents (wherever you may find them) is an important skill for the exceptional leader. Through systematic questioning and talking to your team, you will find obvious connections between certain people and the areas and outcomes that they're most interested in. These are areas they may be able to exert influence. By paying attention to these "matches," you will increase the effectiveness of your delegation and see much more passionate work from people. You will see people go from average to excellent right before your eyes and sometimes do it with amazing speed.

As you make the rounds, if you identify someone whom you cannot see playing any important role in the organization, you must take action. This is a part of leadership that most leaders avoid, but you cannot realistically expect everyone to be on-board and really want to play a meaningful role on your team. You can, and should, expect everyone to be interested in team progress enough to want some real responsibility, though. They should be excited about the opportunity to be a part of something as ambitious as what you're in the process of building. There must be contribution, belief, and enthusiasm.

On an improving team, a single person who refuses to be involved or who makes an effort to ooze cynicism will keep the team connected to the past. A developed leader can't accept that kind of risk. On a high-performance team, the opposite of positive productive energy is not negativism—it's apathy. The good news is that most initially negative people are usually "sellable" and will go from skeptic to advocate with equal passion. You can be patient with them as long as they don't absorb too much attention or energy. This person should be given every possible opportunity to get excited about what's going on. He should be allowed to watch for a short while to be sure that this (and you) are legitimate. If after a reasonable amount of time it becomes clear that he has no real connection to where the team is going, then the team should go on without him.

Building People

Here are eight strategies for leaders who want to be effective people builders and change agents:

1. Everyone absorbs and understands change at their own pace.
2. Skeptics, once they buy in, will usually become advocates.
3. Conflict and misunderstanding can be good, apathy can't.
4. If your changes are properly premeditated, most of the outcomes will be expected and not at all surprising.
5. It's impossible to overestimate how attached people can be to the status quo.

6.   People can be loyal to the company without feeling loyalty to the leader.

7.   You cannot get where you want to go doing things in the same old ways.

8.   At a certain point, not changing is more risky than changing.

There are a couple of other key things for leaders to remember when they're initiating big changes in their organizations:

The future is going to be amazing, *but so is the present*. Right now must be seen as a great place to be in your organization. These are the "good old days." People are proud of the things they've already done. Acknowledging prior progress is a great way to build confidence and add horsepower to new movements. The idea is that "We've done it before, and we'll do it again."

You have to remember that everything affects momentum. You can't allow anything to slow this thing down once it begins to succeed. There's nothing that you can't use to strengthen your vision and the pull of the future. With a little forethought, a leader can be masterful at making any circumstances, even seemingly catastrophic ones, fit into the long-term vision for the team.

If your crew, which is gradually becoming "sold" on the reality of your high-performance, high-challenge, high-involvement vision, sees any lack of resolve in the leader, it will affect them very significantly. It will feed any lingering doubts they have and may make your water-cooler cynic (if he's still there) look very smart. You must be completely bulletproof. In a crisis, you have an excellent opportunity to show poise and resolve. These are your moments of truth. Look forward to them as a way of demonstrating that nothing is more important than what you're trying to build.

☑WELKnote:

It's the leader's primary responsibility to get people in position to succeed in their roles.

Chapter 20 - What Brussels Sprouts and Leadership Have in Common

I'm around 50 years old as of this writing. No matter how old I am, at times my parents still see me as an eight-year-old, maybe even an eighteen-year-old. Recently, I heard my Mom say, "She won't eat Brussels sprouts, she hates them" to my father when we were discussing our dinner plans. I've also heard her say other things that perhaps were true when I was a kid (that I hate beets and parsnips), but are no longer valid.

Let me be clear. I love Brussels sprouts. You'll even find them on the same baking sheet next to the beets and parsnips. If we dine together, I will actually try to convince you to try the Brussels sprouts because I think they have gotten a bad rap all these years.

Which brings me to my point. How many people on your team have gotten a bad rap because you judged them too quickly or too harshly? Or maybe you're continuing to remember them as they were in the beginning of their careers or when they were first promoted into new positions with your company, instead of factoring in their growth over time? It's lazy to fail to see the changes in the people you serve. It's even worse to fail to "coach them up" in areas that you know they need it. You might be thinking, "But I don't have the time to spend with everyone!" I realize this is much easier if you're leading a smaller team, but what do you do if you're working with a large team, or an entire company?

So, who's gotten a bad rap from you? Which team members do you need to circle back on and perhaps rethink their contributions or value to your team? Can't think of anyone? Who are the people you are most frustrated with or disappointed in? Start there. Those people know you're frustrated, and let's assume they're at least trying to develop in the areas you need them to. If you don't think they're at least attempting to improve, is it because they don't think it will change your mind about them anyway? Is there any chance your attitude towards them could lead them to believe you've made up your mind about who they are?

I've been in that position before, needing to improve my skill set to perform at a higher level in my job. I've read a gazillion books, attended tons of seminars, talked to as many successful people as I could, taken classes, gone back to school, etc., trying to improve myself, only to have someone I report to see me as a final product too soon in my career.

I've also had the amazing pleasure to work with people who've had incredible confidence in me, sometimes even when my performance did not warrant it. Those people are the ones that I list when I'm asked about people who've made a difference in my life.

Are you "showing up" for your team? Are you noticing their progress and growth? Are you having growth conversations and laying out specific strategies about what they can do to improve? Have you spent a little time with them painting the picture of what it looks like in the future once they're more competent in their jobs? Are you "futuring" them, noting what their growth looks like in a month, six months, a year, or even ten years? Have you told them about the books you've read or the seminars you have attended that made a difference for you? Are you giving them the tools and the time to make changes? Lastly, are you taking the time to notice if they do?

I love when someone surprises me. I love watching not what people do, but who people *become* in the process. It brings me great joy knowing someone is attempting to learn new skills in order to perform at a higher level.

☑WELKnote:

Take the time to reevaluate and rediscover the people on your team ... and maybe you need to try Brussels sprouts again.

Chapter 21 - Developing a High-Performance Environment

The ability to create and sustain a positive high-performance environment in an organization is one of the master skills of leadership. Despite the indisputable importance of this skill, it's very hard to find practical advice on creating a high-performance atmosphere in our organizations. Everyone seems to agree this ability is the major component of truly exceptional achievement in a team effort over the long term. Why are there so few books, seminars, blogs, and resources dedicated to the development of a high-performance atmosphere? My opinion is that this is a leadership skill that most people believe to be native in a certain kind of leader–an ability that comes naturally to the visionary, charismatic, or motivational leader. Are these skills really so elusive? Can't leaders learn how to develop and manage a high-performance atmosphere for their teams? Of course they can.

Creating a highly charged, super-expectant atmosphere of achievement is not magic; it's effort … and it can be learned. Creating a place where people can be excellent requires that we believe that people will perform at a very high level if we get out of their way and make it our jobs to build them up.

Let's see if we can create this ideal of a high-energy, high-performance, change-ready business atmosphere. We will need to break things down into much smaller pieces to create a recipe that is implementable for leaders with diverse personality types in broadly differing situations.

This high-performance environment we seek is the sum total of all the factors in an organization relating to its culture. It's the combination of history, training, personality, bureaucracy, mission, ethics, compensation, energy, organizational objectives, and access to information. These variables have made the creation of a great atmosphere a seemingly un-trainable part of teambuilding. To add to the confusion, we know that there are people who can manipulate and understand these factors naturally and with almost no effort. I'm not one of these people, so I've had to take great pains to learn this skill in the same way I've learned others, through lots of mistakes and the regret associated with doing it wrong. Maybe I can save you some time and pain. Here's what I've figured out:

The most useful way to think about office/team atmosphere is as "expectation management." The people who succeed in creating and sustaining an excellent high-performance atmosphere are expert expectation managers, and they're extremely sensitive to what their team believes the outcomes will be. People who work with these leaders simply define "good work" differently than those who work for average or unenlightened managers. These exceptional leaders take their optimism and high expectations everywhere they go. To help us get a better grip on this concept, I want to review what this atmosphere is and isn't.

What it is:

- It's the "personality" of your organization.
- It's what people miss when they're away.
- It doesn't *cause* great things to happen; rather, it *lets* great things happen.
- It sets the "speed limit" for your team because it's both a *creator of* and a *result of* expectations that no organization can, for the long-term, rise higher than its atmosphere will allow.
- Atmosphere is vibratory; it's there even when you and your team are not.
- It's the energy of a company, department or office.

What it isn't:

- It isn't measurable, yet it controls everything.

- It isn't in your mission statement.

- It isn't a physical thing. Virtually distributed teams can have great atmospheres.

- It cannot be mandated.

- It isn't physical, but it has a life of its own.

- It isn't in your managers' training manual.

Creating a positive powerful environment in your organization will require a great deal of planning and effort. You will need a strategy for growing it. Remember that atmosphere cannot be altered directly. It's not the result of a campaign, a slogan or an initiative. *It's an effect of many causes.* It's fragile, but it will take on a life of its own if attended to properly.

What follows is the best formula or recipe that I can imagine for creating a highly productive and perceptibly enjoyable team environment in your organization.

Nice People

Common Values

High Expectations

Requisite Skills

Authentic Leadership

Challenging Objectives

=

A Vibrant & Dynamic Environment

I'm hopeful that this recipe does not need much explaining. You will notice that most of the above comes pretty easily, even naturally. The vast majority of people are nice. They have a grounding set of values and would prefer to be in a successful outfit. What needs attention in most organizations are the bottom three requisites, the ones that come from leadership. It's worth noting again that the leader is solely responsible for her organization's atmosphere, even though lots of variables will influence it. She must be extremely, even obsessively attendant to the *meaningful details* that create this high-performance environment. I believe that the office environment is more reliable than a CT scan when it comes to reflecting what's going on in the head of a would-be leader or manager. Your office's "feel" is a direct reflection of your (the leader's) beliefs. Here are a few questions to help you understand your own views on the topic:

- Do you think that business teamwork can be fun?
- Do you believe that your team can accomplish unique and amazing things?
- Do you ever say, "Thank God it's Monday?"
- Are you willing to be emotionally vulnerable to create an atmosphere of trust?
- Do you like your people?
- Can you handle not getting every bit of the credit that comes with a job well done?

If the answer to these questions is yes (or at least maybe), then we're ready to move on to discussing some actual steps to creating your own environment of excellence in your organization or office.

☑WELKnote:

Exceptional Leaders understand the need to manage both the environment and the people.

Chapter 22 - Maintaining a High-Performance Environment

It's certainly more challenging to create a great high-energy environment than it is to maintain one. Any organizational culture, be it good or bad, has its own survival instinct and its own powerful momentum. By thinking of the office environment as the team's "personality," we can see how it would take on a life of its own and be very easy to maintain so long as people are matched well with objectives and the leader is still paying attention.

One of my favorite metaphors for good leadership comes from the sport of curling. Even if you're completely unfamiliar with the sport (as I was), you've probably seen it on TV, maybe during the Olympics. Unofficially, it consists of one team member pushing a really heavy thing hard so it slides down this lane while another team member runs in front of the heavy object with a brush, scrubbing the ice to make the rock move in a straight line and move at a certain speed. The "pushers" are usually really strong and expend a lot of effort just to make the heavy thing go at all. The "brushers" are quick and agile so that they can keep running ahead of the heavy object and keep the path in front of it clear.

In this metaphor, the leader is the person running and sweeping ahead of the sliding object. We make sure that the great efforts of our "pushers" are as successful as they can possibly be. We want to make sure that our pushers look good and that the results of their efforts make them feel that they have accomplished something, even if we have to run and brush ahead of them like maniacs to insure a favorable outcome. That's leadership! When a leader is doing her job, a good portion of her management tactics are just staying out of the way and attending to the details that keep things moving forward. One great leadership trait is being smart enough to know when to do nothing. A great atmosphere takes care of almost everything else.

What follows are some areas needing particular attention to once you have established an environment of excellence in your organization. Some are obvious and some are intangible, but still important:

Environment Deflators:

- Low Expectations of any kind: You must find sources of cynicism and attack. It doesn't matter if these low expectations are stated or implied.

- Softening of Standards: Is the organizational objective comfort or performance? You can't work towards both. If a team is underperforming, everyone should be uncomfortable.

- Ghosts of past failures or past mediocrity: Get rid of anything in your physical or virtual space that can be a reminder of an unproud past.

- Negativism and apathy of any kind: As we have noted, apathy is far more dangerous to your team's general outlook than any negativism could be. Someone who really doesn't care is very unusual. These "bad attitude" people can liven up any conversation and sometimes even represent the majority view. They can say things that others don't want to. Taken in small doses, this person can be a very important part of the organization, especially when you consider that, in most organizations, this person is a veteran who has seen it all and carries significant credibility with your team. Frequently this person will act as a mouthpiece for the dark side. It's far worse if you're leading an organization where nobody ever has anything to say that's out of harmony with the team. That's called a cult or a dictatorship. Neither is good.

- Over-Intervention by the leader: A leader who must be involved in every decision, every dispute, and every happening is not helping his team. Let the group deal selectively with some issues as they come. This is how new leaders rise up. This is how people learn what their capabilities really are. In some organizations, the manager is the only person who gets to think creatively. The rest of the team is just supposed to go by policy or by how they've been trained. By not allowing and applauding flexible and innovative responses, we miss opportunities for growth and the evolution of new answers to old problems. If you think you're the only one with any good ideas in your office, territory, division, or company, you're soon going to notice that the marketplace is able to accept new solutions faster than you alone can come up with them. One mind is not good enough anymore.

Environment Enhancers

- Things that work. Successes and wins are the best recipe for getting more of each.
- True enthusiasts.
- Strategic (on-purpose) diversity. When we talk about diversity these days, everyone thinks about gender, sexual orientation, and race. That should go without saying. I'm talking about diversity in the *kind* of people who are allowed to play a role on your team–the personalities. Managers used to believe that organizational strength came from a spooky kind of like-mindedness among the entire team. "We need to be on the same wavelength," they would say. Well, here's one of those areas where nearly the opposite is true. It seems that the more different kinds of people/personalities you have, the greater the potential strength and energy you will have. The magical friction created by two (or more) completely different viewpoints spawns the best ideas and solutions.

In the old days (ten years ago), groups of suburban 53-year-old white guys would launch products and services and then be amazed at the lack of market enthusiasm or interest. What could they expect? Anything that's conceived in such a narrow frame or perspective cannot really be expected to have a mass-market appeal (except by plain old dumb luck … which does happen).

The next big idea was the focus group. It's easy to imagine how this idea formed. One of the 53-year-old white guys said, "Since we seem to be missing large portions of the market, why don't we bring in representative groups that we can get opinions from?" This idea works in a limited way, but is still far inferior to the concept of your organization actually *being* like the population you're trying to sell to. When services and products are conceived, designed, adjusted, launched, and marketed by the very people who are meant to buy them, the odds of a big hit go up remarkably. If you want to sell to a lot of different kinds of people, you had better BE a lot of different kinds of people.

- A learning leader. At the risk of repeating myself, there's nothing more important in a leader than the perception that you're open to ideas, open to conflict, and open to criticism. The ideal description would be a leader who is a smart, active listener, who is open to communication from any direction or any source, a leader who knows that the best ideas haven't even been hatched yet and who seems to be serene and confident about the success of the enterprise. There's this pervasive sense of "authenticity" about the best leaders. They take more pride in being students of the success process than they would ever take in their positions or titles.

- Optimism.

- Positive recognition of ANY kind. The phrase "catch them doing something right" is one of the most important and meaningful clichés in business.

- Heavy involvement of the team in everything possible. I have never seen "involvement" overdone. Even when certain kinds of participative decision making feels silly, it still counts and has an impact in your organization. How about Sandra the human-resources person helping with the purchase of new office furniture? How about the receptionist reviewing the copy for a new ad you're considering? Should the clerical staff have a voice in choosing a new logo or website layout? Would it make sense to have the techies meet the sales guy you're interviewing? It would seem so, but many of these small involvement opportunities are neglected. Members of teams are denied the right to feel connected to the decision-making in the organization. I would highly recommend that you be on the "overdoing it" side of involvement rather than on the side of neglect.

In the end, the greatest responsibility of a leader is the responsibility of providing a place where people can come to be excellent, to be their best—a place where they can be "caught doing something right." You must create a place where success doesn't surprise anyone, where great expecta-tions greet them at the door and they have a hand in deciding where the team is headed. The atmosphere of your organization can compel people to re-estimate their potential. It's your job to create this high-performance atmosphere, and nothing is more important to you as the leader.

☑WELKnote:

High-performance organizations create an expectation of success.

Chapter 23 - You've Been Promoted!

First of all, congratulations! Being asked to take over a new area of responsibility is a fantastic opportunity for a leader. The situation allows you, possibly for the first time in a long time, to look at things with fresh eyes. Takeover leaders get the kind of objectivity and clear-mindedness that may have been missing in their previous roles. Everyone gets a clean slate, the people on the team and the leader himself. It's a situation built for growth and meaningful improvement.

So why is it that so many leadership transitions fail to meet expectations?

Is it because the people on the team (department, division, etc.) were already working at their peak level before the new leader arrived? Is it because the new leader thought that performance would improve just because she or he showed up? Is it because too little thought was put into what everyone was trying to accomplish with the leadership transition? Or is it because the leader was promoted for a specific set of skills that are NOT even the ones needed in the new job?

The answer can be any of these or a combination of a couple of them. Leadership transitions are a high-stakes game. Typically the new leader has been removed from a team that was performing at a high level (that is how these decisions are usually made), so most transitions involve two teams: the one the takeover leader is leaving behind and the one he or she is being introduced to. Of course, there's a lot of risk in this, and many business leadership transitions are failures in retrospect. They fail for all of the reasons listed above, often spectacularly.

Any management consultant will tell you the rate of leadership transition failures is one of the best-kept secrets in business. And due to the current rate of change of most businesses, we're all moving too fast to do formal transition reviews, succession planning, or even take the time to just look back and see if things worked.

What do we do instead? We make another change. This new era of leadership churn is one of the negative outcomes of our current technology and competition-fueled business environment. Almost nobody is looking to see how these transitions have worked, and most businesses are not gathering the lessons to be gleaned from both failing and successful leadership transitions. The upside? This absence of oversight and review creates a real opportunity for you to do things right. In your leadership transition, you will have an opportunity actually to plan your successful transition, execute your plans, review your success, and make sure people understand why it worked.

Preparing to lead a new team:

Step 1: Clear your mind of any current judgments, biases, and prejudices you already have about this new team. The biggest gift you can give your new team is a clean slate because the non-performers will get a fresh start and the performers will have to keep performing to impress you.

Step 2: Make sure you understand the expectations for this transition. Why is the change being made? Why you? What do we want to happen going forward? How will the success of this transition be judged? You need to know the answers to all of these questions.

Step 3: Make sure that your previous team is being cared for. What will be happening to them? Is it in their best interest? Have you made sure you have publicized their success adequately? Should someone on your former team be considered to take over for you? Have you said your "Thank You's"? Is there something you could do to make sure their transition is successful? Remember, it was your team that got you promoted, not your boss.

Here is what you need to identify, understand, and leverage during your transition. This is the big question: Where is my upside?

Look for:

- Raw talent
- Offices, departments, or divisions trending poorly
- Market opportunities
- People who may be in the wrong role
- Specialists who know how to train

These are your most obvious areas for growth. This is the low-hanging fruit.

Next question: Who on your new team will be brand-new to you?

Is this a team you're familiar with, or are you going to be working with strangers? Brand-new people are a great opportunity for you. Your priorities, communications, and overall leadership style will be fresh with these people, and it will be easier to make an impact. This is another opportunity for you.

Next question: Who are the six to ten people who will determine whether this transition succeeds? And what's in it for them if the transition fails or succeeds? Ignore titles, tenure, and previous performance. There will be a small group of individuals who will be the reason your new team succeeds or fails. It may not be immediately obvious to you who they are. You absolutely need to figure it out before you start making any big plans.

Here are six important considerations to help you think fresh thoughts about your new leadership opportunity:

1. How are you going to raise expectations for your new team?

Doing things in a way your predecessor did not? Fresh approaches. New ideas. New delegations. New ways of thinking about the business you're in. Clear expectations.

2. Choose your numbers carefully.

There are only three or four crucial measures for any business. It does not matter whether we're talking about a single department or a multinational corporation. There will always be just three or four metrics that will tell what is working and what is not. What are they for you?

3. What previous traditions or expectations should you eliminate?

These are things that run on their own inertia. This is the "way we have always done it around here" stuff. It could be reports, meetings, rankings, or social expectations. Some of these things worked at one point, but have pooped out. Some of these things never worked. The easiest way to say that a forward view is more important than history is to cut these things out liberally.

4. Where are you going to get your growth?

This is the hardest part of the planning. There's the hidden upside in your new area of responsibility. Your predecessor could not see it, but it's there. The team members know where the growth opportunities are, so interviewing them will give you some instant clarity. Giving them a platform and asking their opinions will also help you earn "buy in" from your new team. After that, you will need to dig into the numbers and see what they tell you. Inevitably, your growth opportunities will surface.

5. Where will you be firm and where will you be flexible?

This is a way of asking what's important to you. Every leader expects to have to show her teeth occasionally, but you have to pick your moments carefully. There will be a few no-compromise areas, but it cannot be every area or you will lose leverage and credibility.

6.   Go where the response is.

This five-word recommendation can save you years of work if you really understand it. Leaders succeed and fail based on their ability to direct people's energy and attention. Team members will not always agree on that direction. When they don't, the leader will not get the energy and attention he needs to succeed in the project, the initiative, or the business. So go where the response is: Pay attention to who is engaged and "on board" with what you're saying and doing. Trying to change people's minds can be a losing proposition; it puts too much attention on the areas that are not working. Instead, focus your energy on the people who "get it." Make sure they're getting the attention, recognition, and resources to succeed. The others will catch on or they won't, but they will not be the deciding factor in the enterprise.

Being a leader in a takeover role can be a high-wire act. You must premeditate every move. You will be under scrutiny from above and below, so you need to make sure the decisions you're making are an accurate reflection of your priorities and values as a leader. Leverage these recommendations to ensure your success in your new opportunity.

☑WELKnote:

Nothing highlights a leader's strengths and weaknesses like a promotion.

Chapter 24 - Coach Them "Up" or Coach Them "Out"

You did it. After combing through tons of resumes and interviewing everyone who showed an interest, you hired the perfect person for the job. The first few weeks are exciting, even a relief. You immediately trust that your new hire will be able to tackle the new position with complete competence and execution, which happens ... for a while.

Then there are a few missteps, a misunderstanding or two, and finally a royal screw-up. You start thinking that you made a mistake. You *should* have hired the other one. After all, it *was* a tough decision. Come to think of it, you actually even liked the other candidate better. Perhaps he's still available? Maybe you can hire him after all?

Or...

Maybe you're new to your job and you've inherited your team. Everyone seems really eager to please you ... for a while. You're still in the honeymoon phase, but at some point it happens in this situation as well. You come to the same point of needing to find a replacement.

Regardless of how it happens, the scenario is inevitable.

In all of the companies I've consulted with, the first few meetings always include discussions around a few people who are on the proverbial chopping block. I sit and listen to the case for firing them. I immediately have four questions:

1. Why haven't you fired them already?

2. Are you sure they know exactly how to do their jobs?

3. Have you told them everything you're unhappy with about their performance? (I mean a totally honest conversation).

4. Did you give them a plan and a timeline to turn things around?

Do you remember how hard it was when you first started your job? I do. I was qualified, but not confident. Combine the lack of confidence with the lack of communication and you have the makings of a short career. I'm lucky. I had people willing to "coach me up."

Great leaders understand that the honeymoon period is the perfect time to establish the proper expectations for your new hire. It's your responsibility to make sure you coach people up to the expectations you have of them. Their progress does not, will not, and cannot happen without you taking a proactive role.

It's pretty simple. I can't think of very many employees who've ever said, "No, I won't do that," when told what is expected. Most are grateful for the feedback and able to assimilate the information easily.

Your responsibility is to provide the feedback until you decide they *can't* do the job. Coaching them "out" is the process of giving them the necessary feedback until it's crystal clear they cannot and will not be able to perform the job. It's not fair to make the decision they *can't* until you have consistently communicated your expectations.

Coaching them "up" until you coach them "out" will yield growth, change, improvement, and much-needed communication.

☑WELKnote:

The best leaders do not leave performance to chance. Be decisive in your actions. It's your responsibility to make people better or make room for someone new.

Chapter 25 - THE Meeting

I often hear people say they work for a company that doesn't care about them. I always think, "Who is 'the company'?" Whose responsibility is it to make people feel valued? Is it the president, vice president, director of human resources?

Yes. All of the above. We could debate which title in the company should be responsible for making the people feel important, but the truth is anyone and everyone in leadership could and should be thinking about the people who work there. A company can never value people; only the people running the company can value people.

As I write this, my company is going through a culture change. We have people who have been with our company for over thirty years, and we also have a lot of new hires. We have had about a dozen changes at the top in the last ten years, and for the most part, we've survived it all with ease—until now. The thing that is making it more difficult is the employee perception that the company is focusing more on the profits than the people.

The truth is we have to focus more on the profits so we can stay in business. We are not the only company trying to figure out how to do more with less. The cutbacks, layoffs, and cost-management initiatives are actually easier to take than the idea that the people aren't as important as they used to be. It's not true that they aren't valued; it's just not obvious to them that they are. No one is deliberately thinking about the employee experience. I'm not saying no one cares; it's quite the opposite. It's just not obvious to the people who *need* to know they matter. It seems to be a secret in some organizations that having (and keeping) great people is the ultimate competitive advantage.

There are many great examples of corporations fostering a great work environment. Zappos, Google, Quicken Loans, Groupon, Scripps Health, The Container Store, Edward Jones, Intuit, USAA, Southwest Airlines, Transworld Systems, SAS, and QuikTrip, come to mind, as do many others where there's a purposeful effort to enhance the employee experience.

Let's assume you believe you need to make a change. You want to do something about the employee experience. Where do you start? You start with "THE Meeting."

THE Meeting is where you tell others they matter. It's when you stop just talking about the company, and you start talking about the people. It's when you acknowledge that you want to make sure they know how important they are and you actually give your team permission to provide feedback. It's NOT you giving up control or changing directions in how the business runs, it's simply you listening to your biggest customer, the people who provide whatever service your company provides.

Start with a small group–your trusted advisors or your direct reports. Tell them you want to excite the troops. You want to start an employee appreciation campaign, or you want to reinforce the one you already have that's no longer effective. Ask what they think that looks like. You don't have to have all or any of the answers. You just have to ask the right questions of the right people. You might have to spend more time and money than you want, but think of it as an investment. Having a group of dedicated, passionate people working at your organization will come back tenfold. If you have ever spent one dime trying to attract new customers/clients, remember your employees are the best advertising strategy you have.

Get a giant note pad and a bag of markers. Hand out one sheet and marker to each person in the room. Have them brainstorm their ideas for employee appreciation. Give plenty of time to write down as many things as possible. Remember, this might be the first time they've thought of it. You don't want to assign it as homework you want everyone in the room working on the same thing at the same time. The energy for all will lead to a better outcome. Once everyone has a list, pair them up. Have them select their top three ideas from both lists. They have to sell each other and come to consensus.

Then, pair up the pairs until everyone is in one group. Once they all agree on the top three, then decide. Can you take on all three strategies at once? Or should you select one or two from the list to begin with? Make a record of all ideas on the lists. This will give you a list to work from on your timeframe. Perhaps you can do one or two each quarter, and you won't have to have "THE Meeting" to get your ideas. Furthermore, this list is fluid. As the group comes up with more ideas, you can simply add them to your arsenal of potential changes.

Creating the list is the fun, easy part. Executing and continuing the program will require discipline and follow through. If this is not your strength, assign it out, but stay involved. Perhaps you can have a few people from all levels in the organization tasked with suggesting new ideas and keeping the ideas already generated moving forward. The group can be fluid. Select a few mainstays, but allow some rotating members to keep fresh ideas coming in.

Hear this: If you never execute one thing on the list, giving people a voice can be the change that is needed. I'm not advocating blowing smoke at people and "acting", I'm saying that even if your budget won't allow some of these strategies to be implemented, you will still make them feel valued by listening to their ideas.

What will surprise you most is how simple the things are on the lists that you will witness. It really takes so little to make people feel appreciated and valued.

Here are a few activities that I have seen of these lists:

- Pizza parties
- Bowling leagues
- Contests
- Domestic partner benefits
- Flex time
- Suggestion boxes
- Being "in the know" on upcoming changes
- Involvement in executive decisions
- Coffee service provided
- Movie tickets
- Dinner gift certificates
- Focus group participation
- Hand-written thank-you cards
- Birthday parties
- Trips

Paying attention to the perception of your employees yields a better work atmosphere, more loyal employees, and more customers, which all lead back to more profits. Remember, people can always find another job, but they may not find another place where they feel like they matter.

☑WELKnote:

Exceptional leaders look for big and small opportunities to enhance their employees' work experience.

Chapter 26 - Be Big for Your People

Picture this... A superhero wearing blue tights and a red cape, with a big puffy chest, oversized chin in the air, a disproportionate amount of jet black hair piled high, but combed straight back. He leans forward on one leg, one hand on his hips, the other pointing in the air, and a bubble above his head saying ... "I'm here to save the day!"

Isn't that the perfect picture of a leader? NO! Actually, "Being Big" would be the exact opposite of that description. It's probably not even detectible in the ways that are the most defining. You could call it the softer side of leadership, but you would be wrong to think that means weakness. I'm talking about the kind of leadership that elicits loyalty, commitment, respect, inspiration, dedication, and top performance. It offers team members security in knowing the leader "has their back." They know no matter what happens, you're always there for them. Whether it's to cheer them on or kick their butts, you consistently show up.

Let's cover a few ways exceptional leaders can be big.

1. **They don't use singular possessive pronouns**. One of the best ways to tell if leaders have evolved is how they share credit with other people. Do they use "we" and "our" pronouns? Or are they always saying "me" and "my"? The minute you use a singular possessive pronoun as a leader, you're putting yourself above the people you lead. That's a sign of an undeveloped leader, and it will create a chasm between you and your team that will be hard to overcome. Continued over time, it will create resentment and ultimately diminish your effectiveness. Your people will always play

a part in your success, and making sure you continue to recognize that will create more loyalty and job satisfaction for your team.

2. **They step aside and give their people the limelight.** This isn't always easy to do. After all, you played a part in their success, right? You want some credit too, right? While you probably deserve it, you can never be the one demanding it. Here's the truth. Continuing to remind someone how unpolished he was in the beginning or taking credit for someone's success can only diminish your effectiveness with top performers. It's okay to reminisce occasionally about how far someone has come, but your job is to talk about the future and to continue to paint a bigger picture for their success. If you don't, top people will outgrow you. Worse, they won't value your influence any more. Creating a platform for your people to shine is a great gift you can offer your people. Any attempt to elevate yourself instead will be construed as arrogant or insecure. It will also set up a competition. They will be trying to prove they could do it without you, and you will be attempting to prove they couldn't. It's quite silly when you think about it. If you always try to make sure you get credit for things, you'll never gain the total trust of your people. Ever. I can tell you that having one of my team members say "Thank you" or comment in any way that I've assisted them in their success is the greatest gift of leadership. It's the ultimate "Be Big" feeling for me.

3. **They are secure.** Once you're leading the team, it's implied that you're valued and your worth is established. Many leaders try to justify their promotion, and they don't need to. You were promoted for a reason. *Own* that. Rely on your own evaluation as opposed to giving your power to those that might not see the bigger picture. While it's a good idea to solicit feedback, that doesn't mean you

should be defined by it. Integrate it with what your own truth is. Ultimately, aging helps us all figure out that what other people think of us is really none of our business. We also learn whom we should and shouldn't listen to.

4. **They tell the truth**. That goes for policy and performance. They answer tough questions without a lot of fluff and aren't afraid of other people's reactions. Often the leader is tasked with delivering news that will create a change for the team. Perhaps it's a price increase, a new bonus structure, an increase in quota, a violation of the dress code, etc. Whatever it is, be prepared for potentially volatile conversations, but never avoid them. Your ability to deliver and lead people through change will be easier if you can cut through the fog and just tell the truth. People respond better to change when the leadership is confident and transparent. They don't respond well when they're left in the dark or someone seems apologetic about the situation.

They also tell the truth about performance. I recently consulted with a company that let a top person go because he wasn't effective in his role. I asked what that meant and was told, "He was taking on too much work in the plant and not doing enough of the administrative part of his position." I asked how he responded to the initial conversation explaining he was falling short, and there was dead silence. "Well, he just should have known that." Really? How should he have known that? Don't ever assume top performers know what your expectations are. It's all too common that we unknowingly set people up to fail. We think they're smart enough to figure it out, and then we're upset when they don't. You can't hesitate to coach them just because of their title or past performance. No matter how good they are, they can be better. Leaving top performers alone because "they don't need any hand holding" is a mistake. Only leaders with nothing to offer could justify that point of view. Even then, you would be smart to stay more connected so you can learn from them.

Lastly, those top performers provide the best opportunity for growth in your company and on your team. They will be able to integrate feedback faster than you can get non-performers to overcome inertia.

5. **They understand how to manage up**. We've covered dealing with your team, but what about the people you report to? Sometimes it's smart to make sure your wins are visible to those deciding your future. If you aren't tooting your own horn, who will? I'm lucky. I have some amazing business partners that I know have my back. I know when I miss the mark, they'll tell me. When I'm over the line, they'll nudge me back to center. When I'm under attack, as we all are at one time or another, they come to my defense. They won't let my body of work or reputation be devalued by a misstep here or there. By the way, you know who you are, and thank you.

   If you aren't as lucky, you'll have to make sure you "sell" yourself, not in an obnoxious conversation about how amazing you are, but through a strategic one that addresses what you're focusing on and what your priorities are. Put together a snapshot of your victories. Check in with your superiors (I hate that term, but it captures the point here) and make sure you're meeting their expectations. Never forget that the best way to promote your success is by promoting the performance of your people. Having top performers on your team is the best reflection of exceptional leadership.

6. **Saving the best for last, the best way to Be Big for your team is for you to continue to grow as a person and as a leader**. Your number-one client is the people you lead. Their growth and

success are tied to yours. Stay curious. Learn all you can about your company, your services, your market, your industry, and your team. Don't just know enough to get the job done. Know more and do more than is required. I've seen leaders get to the top, not realizing the ladder never ends. More rungs will be added and more people will be vying for the coveted positions. Don't get lazy. Don't get comfortable. Don't ever think you have arrived. Your best today will be expected tomorrow. Your people and your teams will continue to get better, and so should you.

There are many more examples of how you could grow as a leader. This entire book was written in an attempt to further answer this question. Read on!

☑WELKnote:

There are multitudes of meaningful ways for leaders to inspire their people.

Chapter 27 - Promoting Top Producers

The best players usually aren't the best coaches. Think about the golfer who has a natural swing or the baseball player who gets a great jump on the ball, or maybe even the tennis player with a 120 mile-an-hour serve. Is it nature or nurture? Let's not debate and just agree that it can be both. They had some ability and then worked their tails off to hone their skills.

How about you? How did you get promoted? Were you a top producer at your company? Was your promotion based on performance, or were you promoted because of your ability to cultivate and nurture the abilities of those around you?

Now, let's take a closer look at the high producer and what happens when you put her in a leadership role. The hardest part of coaching is relating to the "inability" of people. In other words, a great player hasn't had to think deeply about the basic mechanics of the sport after becoming proficient.

Noel Burch's *The Four Stages of Learning* lay out the blueprint for learning new things. We will talk more about this later in the book, but the idea is that any attempt to learn something new goes through these four stages:

Stage 1- Unconscious Incompetence. You don't know what you don't know. It's actually a great state to be in. Oblivion. No awareness.

Stage 2- Conscious Incompetence. This is the worst stage of all. You now know that you don't know. You're fully aware that you're not good at something.

Stage 3- Conscious Competence. You know it and you can do it, but you really have to think about it. It's a two-step process.

Stage 4- Unconscious Competence. You know it and you can do it without even thinking. It's second nature.

Great players walk around mostly in stage four of their chosen sports. When those same players have to coach people who are in stages one, two, or three, they will have a very difficult time.

It's hard to remember the details of stage two once you've passed it. The great coach not only remembers it, but is also able to relate to the experiences of the people working towards stage four. He teaches them from "where they are" in the process of learning, instead of expecting them to be in stage four. He has "relatability" along with the ability to provide step-by-step instructions to get there because the only way to get to stage four is awareness and practice.

The leader who can stay connected to the mind and experience of the employee/learner will be successful. The leader who just keeps expecting people to "be better" or "do better" will burn through people and not cultivate the potential of those they serve.

You must be able to create a process by which your people can succeed. I see this as one of the fundamental downfalls of very talented people who are promoted: their inability to be relatable. If you're unconsciously competent and not able to connect to the conscious incompetence of your people, you will not be an effective leader. They need four things from you to get to stage four: vision, a plan, repetition, and a cheerleader.

The Vision

This is simply crystalizing what your team members bring to the organization. It's not a mission statement or a daylong seminar; it's helping people see themselves as an integral part of the team and creating that picture of what it looks like when they're "up to speed." What difference will they make to the overall picture?

The Plan

What exactly is needed for them to be more proficient in their position? Is it research? Talking to other employees? Studying? Talking to clients? Reading internal memos? Also, what *is* a reasonable time line for their learning curve?

Repetition

Practice doesn't make perfect; it makes permanent. If you don't meet regularly with your people and give them the feedback, they will just get better at doing it wrong. You must provide constructive criticism and have the crucial conversations needed to move people to stage four.

Cheerleading

What? You didn't sign up to be a cheerleader? You don't have the time or the patience to get people up to speed? Then you have two options: Surround yourself with very competent people who can serve as a buffer and help you, or continue to lose great people to other opportunities. This might seem harsh, but the most important job of a leader is to develop other people. Spending time helping other people grow in their positions is the true job description of leadership. The payoff? Parlaying your knowledge and finding the right people who can grow the company creates infinite possibilities. It will provide exponential growth. Not doing it is one of the reasons leaders and companies fail.

Who needs more attention? Who comes to mind when you think about someone not living up to the potential you saw in him when he was hired? What is your role in his trajectory or lack thereof?

Perhaps you have a few calls to make. I know I do.

☑WELKnote:

Exceptional leaders have to learn how to coach effectively and how to recognize progress when they see it.

Chapter 28 - Understanding the Difference Between Can't and Won't

Managing successfully through disappointing performances can be one of the toughest aspects of leadership. Leaders who routinely carry their expectations high are bound to be disappointed, but the ability to manage this kind of disappointment is a necessary skill for any leader intent on building a high-performance team.

We confront the most challenging disappointments when real business results are at odds with our personal expectations. Most leaders develop the ability to read people and accurately project their potential. The disappointments of being wrong about someone's capabilities or intentions can be especially hard to accept.

Leaders get reputations for how they routinely deal with these kinds of disappointments. Some managers will not alter their high hopes for a person regardless of the amount of performance evidence that contradicts these expectations. We have all worked with managers like this. They end up with a reputation for not being able to see people critically. They're often seen as weak performance evaluators, or worse, as Pollyannas.

At the other end of this spectrum are those managers who because of their repeated disappointments with people overcorrect in the other direction–they become cynical about people and what they're capable of. They consciously lower their estimation of what people can do. Having negative expectations insulates these managers against disappointments. Everyone reminds them of someone else who let them down. Poor performances serve only to confirm their low expectations. It's easy to see how this cycle can continue for these people-weary and cynical leaders.

Exceptional leaders are not polarized or prejudiced by their experiences with the people they lead. They develop their expectations for people through both qualitative and quantitative judgment. When they're wrong about a person's capabilities or intentions, they approach the issue with the goal of improving the situation or learning from it. This is where a complete understanding of the difference between a "can't" and a "won't" can really help.

You have a performance issue to resolve. You need to get to the root of the problem in order to successfully act on it. There's always a bottom-line performance issue underneath all of the extraneous issues usually addressed in business settings: Is it the *capability* of the person you were wrong about, or were you wrong about his *intentions?* Just knowing the answer can make all of the difference when you're trying to manage through disappointing performances.

The fundamental question is this: Is it a *can't* or a *won't?* We need to know this as leaders because the very different answers lead to correspondingly different solutions.

This applies to the following performance issues:

- A new salesperson who has not made his target number of prospecting calls in either of his first two weeks with the company
- A district manager who has not organized effective planning meetings for her team
- An administrative assistant who is always ten minutes late to staff meetings
- A call center representative who can't seem to answer the phone before the fourth ring
- A staff accountant who has turned in sloppy and inaccurate reports several times this year
- A regional vice president whose annual business plan does not

contain any of the initiatives identified as top priority by senior management

- A consultant who never follows presentation scripting that has proven to be effective
- A territory manager who routinely underperforms against his budgeted plan

The examples include anywhere there are unexplained performance deviations or outcomes that seem contrary to what you, as the leader, expected. Remember, your high expectations of your team members will be the strongest positive factor in influencing successful behavior. Exceptional leaders should only get surprised "down" at low performance, not "up" at successful outcomes.

John is a new account executive on the team. His action plan calls for him to make 200 prospecting calls in each of his first four weeks. This 40-per-day prospecting pace will allow him to schedule a full week of sales presentations. In over 20 years of watching ratios for new people, the company has determined that when new salespeople make their 200 calls each week, they will set a solid selling schedule and close enough business to be successful in the difficult early stages of a sales career. The company is so confident in this plan that they even discuss it during the interview to make sure they don't hire someone who does not understand the value of heavy prospecting activity at the beginning of a sales career.

John is in his third week after his initial training. In his first week after training, he made 137 calls and set four sales appointments. In week two, John made 157 calls and set three appointments. At the end of each of those weeks, John's manager reminded him of the 200-call benchmark and how risky it is to try to succeed with a weak selling schedule. To make matters worse, John has confided in his manager that he's nearly broke and needs to start selling fast.

The manager is confused. This seemingly intelligent guy says he needs to do well, but is ignoring the most important success guideline he's been given. The manager schedules time to talk with John early in week three.

"John, I'm concerned with your progress so far. You've fallen short in each of your first two weeks. I know you're very aware of our target–200 calls per week for your first month. Yet you've decided to do less than that each week. I think you're an intelligent and capable person, and that's why I wanted you on this team in the first place. Here is the question I need you to answer: Are you not making the 200 calls because you can't or because you won't?"

This question will not be answered quickly or without care because both possible answers keep the problem squarely on the shoulders of the listener. There's no opportunity to thrust responsibility back at the manager or the company. If it's a "can't," then the capability of the person needs to be addressed. Is it a training issue? Is he the wrong person for the job? Is there some issue keeping him from being able to perform?

If the answer is a "won't," then we're really talking about intentions, which really means the basic relationship between the person and the company. A "won't" may mean that there's a real breach in the agreement between this person and the company.

The can't/won't question will help you navigate through some of your more vexing people issues. The answer to this very direct either-or inquiry will at the least give you a solid stance for understanding, and solving, key performance shortcomings in your organization.

☑WELKnote:

The ability to be direct and ask the right questions is another cornerstone trait for exceptional leaders.

Chapter 29 - Don't Your People Deserve Your Great Expectations?

Have you ever been disappointed by someone you hired or promoted? Have you ever thought "There's no way he can make it," but you had to hire him anyway because he was the best you could find? Or have you hired someone with some skepticism who ended up being a valued member of your team? How many people have truly surprised you?

We've all had that person who gave us a shot of confidence at just the right time. Perhaps it was a parent, a coach, or even a mentor who made a timely comment or treated us in a way that made us know we were special, someone who said, "You can do better and I expect you to," and these few words served to ignite your own burning desire to succeed.

I overheard a conversation once between two strangers attempting to make small talk.

"I missed my flight and won't make it in time for my son's game tonight."

"I'm sorry to hear that. Is his team any good?"

"They have only lost one game so far."

"Is your son a good football player?"

"Well, he sure thinks he is. He keeps saying he's going to get a football scholarship to the University of Oklahoma. I keep telling him he's just going to be disappointed and needs to quit thinking he's going to get paid to play football. There are so few guys who make it to that level."

"I hear ya. It's pretty tough. What position does he play?"

"Nose guard. Do you know how hard it is to get a scholarship as a nose guard?"

"Nearly impossible."

At this point, my curious brain started churning. How hard IS it to get a scholarship as a nose guard? Is it harder than the right tackle? Is he any good? What kind of degree does want to earn? Does he want to go to an Ivy League school, but his dad is pushing him to State U? Maybe he won't make Division I, but I wonder if he could play for a Division II school? What does a nose guard really want to be when he's out of college? I can't remember ever meeting someone who was a nose guard. Who was the nose guard on our team?

Then the next question ….

"How old is he?"

Wait for it ….

"Eleven."

I truly jumped out of my seat and turned around to see what the kind of person who would destroy a kid's dream at the age of eleven looked like. I was stunned. Two guys who looked like they were in fairly good shape and probably even played "back in the day" were agreeing how silly the eleven-year-old was for thinking he could make it at the college level. I was really dumbstruck. What should I say to them? Don't I owe it to the eleven-year-old to at least comment about how they were being unfair to squash his dreams at such a young age? Do they have any idea how unfair it is to throw in the towel on someone before he's even twelve years old?

I started to say something, but instead I stared and didn't say a word. I didn't trust myself to say it in a way that wouldn't come out like, "Hey, just because you two are losers and didn't make it doesn't mean he can't!" That was, after all, the only thing that came to mind.

I thought about that exchange for the rest of my flight. At what age *should* we give up on people? I hope you can't even read that without thinking, "Never!" Our job as leaders (and coaches and parents) is to promote the *possibilities* of our people, not the *probabilities* of the population at large. I don't care what personality test you give or how long you've been hiring, someone will always surprise you.

It's easy to be excited when someone is new. But how do you feel after a few weeks, or months, or years? It's inevitable that person will let you down in one way or another. A "manager" might just fire him or give up on him. But an exceptional leader? That leader will recognize the learning curve. He won't decide or change his mind about people's value after a single event or comment. He will be able to integrate people's progress over time into the overall view of their importance to the company or the team. He will know that mistakes will be made, but he won't let a few missteps define someone's contributions. Most importantly, he will take ownership in the success AND the failure of his employees.

I'm not advocating saving everyone. Jim Collins wrote beautifully in *Good to Great* about getting the right people on the bus, but some people just have not been given the right set of circumstances for success. Perhaps no one has ever been patient enough or caring enough to give them the grace they needed to learn how to be successful. These are the kinds of circumstances that true leaders can give their team members by helping instill confidence in them. It might even mean recognizing when someone is in the wrong job and instead of firing him, putting him in a different position.

Exceptional Leaders know that every person has the capacity to change and grow. They know we are never a final product, and they inspire their teams to continue to develop. A leader might be inclined to take credit for the talented people she hires, but the real test is how she holds herself accountable for how a team develops. Being able to see and cultivate the potential in every person you work with is the mark of great leadership.

The father in the story? He's missing a great opportunity to teach his son about commitment and perseverance. He could tell his son stories of great athletes who were short on talent but long on desire who have gone on to be great in their chosen sports. He could give examples of college football "walk-ons" who now play in the NFL. He could have talked about Abraham Lincoln's many failures before being elected President. He could have told him a thousand other stories of people who beat the odds and went on to great personal and professional success.

Which brings us to this: Have you given up on someone? Does that person deserve it? Who on your team right needs a second chance, or maybe needs to be in a different position? Are you overlooking someone? Who needs a little confidence from you to propel them in their position? Whom have you taken for granted or pigeon-holed with a certain skill set? Have you forgotten about someone? Who was on the other end of a snap judgment you made about their talent or capability? Whom do you need to view with fresh eyes?

Take another look. They deserve it.

☑WELKnote:

Leaders are in the expectations business. They learn to see the upside in people and situations.

Chapter 30 - Leadership = Paying Attention

Many progressive books on leadership correctly identify *positive recognition* as one of the most powerful means a leader has to influence results. Leaders who take the time to recognize where success is happening on their teams will always out-produce leaders who focus on what is broken or what is not working with their teams. This is Leadership 101, yet many would-be leaders just don't get it. Often, it's because they themselves have never had an opportunity to work with a leader who learned the necessary sensitivity and skills to lead positively.

Many underachieving managers think of positive recognition as a "soft skill." They think it's something that serious business leaders and high-level executives can leave to someone else. Exceptional leaders don't accept this view. They know how to influence people and action with recognition. They know that positive attention being paid to success is the best way to: make sure their successful people know they're valued, make sure that whatever is succeeding continues, and clearly and strongly influence the behavior of the people who are not succeeding.

As we discussed previously, the ability to recognize success and "catch people doing it right" is at the forefront of all leadership attributes. It's central to the desire to reinforce positively actions that we, as leaders, want to see repeated by the people on our teams. Unenlightened or under-skilled leaders tend to focus on the things that their team members don't know and the actions they're not taking, thus reinforcing these failing images in the minds of the people.

While the ability to be able to provide constructive comments is important, these must be balanced with recognition. Any leader who can become good at identifying the actions that lead to long-term success will see the team consistently develop as he builds positive, reinforcing relationships with them.

It's our job to look for what we have come to call "Success Events." These are the many little and big things that happen along the way when someone is learning to succeed in a particular role. These events break down into three general categories: (1) performance events (successful outcomes), (2) demonstrations of effort, and (3) exhibitions of attitude and commitment.

Performance Events

This is the easiest area to pay attention to because this category focuses on results. Every kind of successful result should be recognized. Depending on your situation, results would be sales, customer service victories, documented improvements, client commendations, hitting or exceeding desired targets, cost savings, promotions, landmarks, and every other kind of positive outcome. Most companies make an effort to recognize performance–they just don't take it far enough. Usually firms recognize only efforts having a direct effect on revenue or customer satisfaction. There are specialists and role-players all over your organizations doing a great job every day who would be sorely missed if they were no longer part of the team, even if they're in low-profile jobs. Does your office have a receptionist who is never late? You would certainly notice if he were constantly late, but how about some recognition for reliability? Does your website function perfectly? Someone is responsible for that. Does your mailroom run like clockwork? Who's responsible for that excellence? How about payroll or HR? Paying attention to solid performance is never a mistake. Look for it on all levels, and do not let people fade into the background just because they have been on the team for a long time.

Effort Events

These are the "cause" part of the cause-and-effect equation in any organization. As leaders, we should pay attention to efforts that we know will lead to meaningful results. The results are usually obvious to everyone, so being tuned in to the *efforts* our team members are making is a key leadership element.

An important sale, a key improvement, or an exceptional customer interaction is always the result of some special effort make by a committed individual. It's especially important to recognize quality effort when the result is not clear to everyone. Often teams do not accurately connect the effort and the eventual result. As a leader tuned in to your team's effort, you will not let this happen. Other clear examples of sincere effort are participation in office work, team members working on themselves through seminars or continuing education, staying late or arriving early, aiding someone outside their department—anything above and beyond a person's norm should be acknowledged. Remember, intelligent effort or an "above-and-beyond" contribution should always be recognized.

Attitude and Commitment Events

These are actions that convey people's belief in themselves and their commitment to the team. They are not always obvious, so leaders must have their antennae set to catch these kinds of recognition opportunities. They're easy to miss, and yet they're very important. Some good examples of attitude and commitment events are: taking responsibility for something outside of your department, a very enthusiastic interaction with a client, someone talking to the right influences, written goals, heavy involvement in a meeting, encouraging a friend or relative to apply for a job in your organization, offering up creative ideas, attending a seminar or meeting that requires an investment of time or money and many, many (many) others.

Providing a place where people can be excellent means that we must all learn the art of recognition. A timeless and unbreakable rule of management is *what gets rewarded, gets repeated.* If that was the only leadership idea you knew, you could succeed as a leader and team developer. Many aspiring leaders do not succeed because they never grasp this rule. It's interesting to note that the phrases we all use to describe these positive actions sound as though they're actually describing some kind of financial compensation: "paying" attention, "spending" time, "rewarding" with recognition. This is no accident. Recognition is an important part of how we compensate people for their efforts at work. Many studies over the years have shown that most people rate positive recognition as more important than financial compensation when discussing job satisfaction.

Those of us who forget to pay positive attention to people or can't find anything good to say are, in fact, saying plenty. There are great things going on in your organization. If not, then it's your job as the leader to create headlines yourself. Make paying attention the number-one item on your job description.

☑WELKnote:

Leaders understand that there are many ways for people to contribute and make the effort to recognize as many of them as possible.

Exceptional Leaders Know Why People Do What They Do

Chapter 31 - Introverted & Extroverted Leaders

When most people think about being introverted or extroverted, they usually think about how other people come across when they meet them. Are they shy or outgoing? Do they talk a lot, or are they quiet? While that may offer a clue, it's definitely not the litmus test for whether someone has an introverted or extroverted interaction style.

The true definition of *introvert* or *extrovert* lies in these two questions:

1. How does someone process information?
2. Where does her energy come from?

If you think about introverts and extroverts in those terms, instead of whether someone is always talking or being quiet, you begin to shift how you interact with the population at large.

Extrovert Characteristics

Extroverts have a one-step process for thinking and speaking. They speak while attempting to form their points of view. Extroverts are often fast-paced. They process information out loud because they have an external thinking process. When you ask an extrovert a question, what do you typically get? You get *an* answer. Eventually you get *the* answer, but not without hearing everything that pops into his mind first.

For example, you call your extroverted spouse after a long day at work and ask a simple question: "Where do you want to have dinner tonight?" Without missing a beat, you hear, "I don't care, well, I'm really in the mood for a steak tonight, so let's go to McGill's ... I've also been wanting to try that new restaurant downtown on Boston Avenue, but I bet there's going to be a long line ... I haven't had Mexican food in a long time, so let's run over to On The Border... but I'm trying to lose some weight so ... let's eat fish ... the truth is I'm kind of tired, I'll just pick up something on the way home and we can have dinner in tonight."

If you're the person listening, you're thinking that you're going to McGill's for steak, then you're going to the new restaurant on Boston Avenue, then you're going for fajitas, then sushi, only to end up eating at home.

With an extrovert, you hear the processing that leads them to the answer. You hear it in real time, at the same time they're thinking about it. They think and speak in a one-step process.

I love listening in on two extroverts in a conversation. They banter back and forth, cutting each other off, talking more and more loudly, and no one's feelings get hurt. The best way to know that an extrovert is interested in what's being said is that he's interrupting you while you're speaking. You said something that triggered a thought, and he blurts it out while you're talking. The truth is, an interruption from an extrovert is really a sign of interest!

Of course, social norms tell extroverts interrupting is rude, so they try to stay quiet. That causes them to start thinking about what they want to say instead of listening, only to be told they aren't good listeners. They can't win!

For the person listening to the extrovert, it can feel like being on a rollercoaster. The conversation is usually at a quick pace with highs and lows, sudden twists and turn, and usually a few surprises. The worst part in the exchange occurs when your question is initially answered with the first thing that comes to mind, and it ends up hurting your feelings.

So let's play this out: The extrovert keeps saying the first thing he thinks, and it causes hurt feelings or arguments. Over time, the extrovert begins to hold back and learns to be quiet so no one will be upset with him. This ultimately leads to a slow withdrawal from the relationship. He doesn't trust himself to say it "right," and then he doesn't trust the receiver to give him some grace, so there's no other way to avoid the conflict.

The first thing extroverts say is not how they truly feel. It's merely the first thing *associated* with the conversation. The introverts probably have the same associations in many situations, but their comments come after they have thought it through. If you're introverted, let me ask you this: "What if you actually said everything you thought about?" Can you imagine the trouble you would be in? That's the world of an extrovert!

If you're an extrovert and you say something you know is inappropriate, just follow it with, "I need a pass on that. I said that because that was the first thing that I thought of, but it's not really how I feel." It doesn't always work, but it's definitely a show of strength and value in the relationship with the listener.

Extroverts Gather Energy Externally

Being around people and having external stimulation typically energizes extroverts. They are typically very kinesthetic. They are highly mobile and love being where the action is.

They enjoy group activities, talking to strangers, interacting with different kinds of people, and usually entertaining the group. Remember, interaction is the fuel for them, so they need the engagement.

Things that would be stressful for the extrovert would include:
- Not being able to give an opinion
- Isolation from others
- People who are not open
- Not being heard
- Being left out or excluded
- Silence

- Extended time alone
- Keeping it all inside
- Lack of interaction
- Being ignored

Introvert Characteristics

Unlike the extrovert, the introvert processes things internally before he speaks. Remember how asking an extrovert a question means you get to hear everything she thinks? Not so with an introvert.

Ask introverts a question and you often get "the stare" or silence. They begin processing the question silently, and you often don't get to hear the process.

Let's go back to the dinner question. "Where do you want to have dinner tonight?" The introvert will begin to think. He or she might even say, "I don't care" to buy a little time, but maybe she is *thinking*, "I'm really in the mood for a steak tonight so maybe McGill's … I've also been wanting to try that new restaurant downtown on Boston Avenue, but I bet there's going to be a long line … I haven't had Mexican in a long time, so perhaps we should run over to On The Border. I really need to lose weight, though, so maybe we should do the new sushi restaurant." Then she might finally say, "The truth is I'm kind of tired, I'll just pick up something on the way home and we can have dinner in tonight."

Now, the time it takes to get to the answer is the same, but because the introvert does it in silence, it seems longer. Unfortunately, extroverts mistake the silence as an invitation to start talking about the options.

I'll let you in on a secret that all introverts know: Their extroverted partners are impatient and won't honor their silent process. They know that if you ask a question and you're not willing to wait for the answer, they shouldn't bother spending the energy to think about it because you're going to make the decision and move on anyway. Knowing this saves them time and energy.

By the way, I'm not talking about a question they have heard before or a question they know the answer to off the tops of their heads. Introverts will answer those questions as quickly as any extrovert. I'm talking about things they need to ponder or questions requiring some thought.

And why is this even important? It's important because our society has conditioned us to value the person who has the quick answer over the one who needs more time. In many cases, we are truly missing the gifts the introverts bring to our workplaces. Our unwillingness to honor internal processing or let some time pass between comments compromises the input of introverts.

Think about the leader who throws out a question and says, "I value your input, and not only do I value it, but I am willing to wait without tapping my fingers or sighing for your point of view."

I have a very introverted business partner, and I have learned a few strategies that work best for us to get the most out of our partnership. I never run into his office and say, "Look, I need an answer right now." If I do, I'm going to get a compromised response from him. He's going to try to give me an answer quickly because he's trying to get me the information I need on my time frame instead of his. By creating that urgency, I have put him under an unbelievable amount of stress.

A better option is to email him or Instant Message him and say, "I need to talk about the travel schedule for the upcoming speaking engagement next week—when you're ready." The times that I don't do that and walk in demanding answers, I literally watch him start spinning in his chair. He won't even look me in the eye because he's trying to gather his thoughts. He's doing whatever he can to buy himself the few seconds that he needs so he can engage in the conversation and be fully present.

By the way, he wasn't sitting there waiting on me to come in. He was fully involved in something else. My expectation that he respond quickly is unreasonable at best. For me to give him that time is definitely the way I honor his process.

I also give him an agenda before meetings so he can gather his thoughts. I know he likes to write down his deliverables so he can make sure we address his needs as well as mine.

Lastly, I try to be quiet when it's his turn to talk. (That one is the hardest!) By the way, this is not nearly as awkward as it sounds or reads. It's just being aware that pauses are not invitations for me to talk.

Introverts Gather Energy Internally

Introverts gather their energy internally. Typically, non-stop interaction exhausts the introvert. They are most likely to interact in small groups and typically enjoy their time being alone.

Introverts don't usually like work cubicles where they're invited to hear everything their neighbors are saying and often prone to being dragged into impromptu conversations.

Other things that are stressful for introverts might include:

- Non-stop interaction
- Being put on the spot
- No privacy
- Meeting new people
- Socializing in groups
- Interruptions
- Invasion of space
- Small talk or chit-chat
- Group activities
- Too much public affirmation

The bottom line is we are all somewhere on the continuum of the introvert/extrovert scale. I'm sure you saw yourself in both of the descriptions, as some of this is situational. The real point is to begin understanding your predisposition. What is learned for you, and what comes more naturally? What truly gives and what takes your energy?

Examining the answers can mean the difference between ending the day energetically or barely being able to drive home.

☑WELKnote:

Understanding your personal interaction style, whether you are extroverted or introverted, is a big step towards being an Exceptional Leader.

Chapter 32 - Leveraging Your Introverted Leadership Style

You seem cool, calm, and collected. People think you're either very wise or completely oblivious to what is going on, but we both know you aren't. In a society that values the fast talker, the first to speak, the one holding court at the front of the room, let's agree that this short-sided point of view misses the gifts of an introverted leader.

Since introverts think before they speak, it stands to reason that most introverted leaders aren't usually the first to speak up in many situations. Probably the biggest complaint your team has is they don't know what you're thinking or they aren't sure how you feel about a situation. Take someone that is a bit insecure and add reduced feedback, and you might have a potential problem.

If you're an introverted leader, you have been set up by the extroverts who immediately say whatever is on their minds and are quick to offer feedback. We are conditioned to associate immediate feedback with successful leadership, even though there's truly no correlation.

I promise I'm not about to try to convince you to start saying everything that comes to mind, but let's discuss some strategies that can comfort your team and still honor your interaction style.

Your leadership style can seem more empathetic than that of your extroverted counterparts because introverts are usually good listeners. Since you aren't one to jump in and interrupt, people feel "heard." Often people will comment about how you really seem interested in understanding their point of view (They don't need to know that you muted the phone and are doing emails during the call; nor will we mention here that this is actually one of your strategies). Who doesn't like someone who will listen to all of the "noise" that can happen for the employee?

You can also be relied on to provide well-thought-out responses. There aren't many off-the-cuff comments coming from you, and your ability to think things through before you deliver any news to the group is one of your true strengths. Being able to filter the information and provide the appropriate comment is comforting and can calm the biggest of storms.

Your need for a little time to reflect and think through a situation lends itself to honoring the time others need as well. Not demanding immediate feedback and giving others the space to process their own thoughts is welcomed by the introverts you serve.

But all of the amazing patience you seem to possess can actually backfire as well. Not providing the feedback can end up looking like you're withholding essential information from the team, and it might be keeping employees up at night. There's certainly a balance to the dissemination of information. Too much can be an overshare, but too little leaves room for people to make up their own stories, which can be dangerous at best.

Typically, one of the toughest tests for introverted leaders is the demand for on-the-spot answers. Let's review your "Introvert Miranda Rights."

"You have the right to remain silent. Anything you say can and will be used against you in the court of public opinion. Should you choose to give up this right, you risk unnecessary exposure of the information you provide and the energy you will undoubtedly exert."

Don't you love having permission to actually think? I'll go a step further and say you need to make sure you schedule time to think. Turn off the phone and shut down the email at least once a day. It's up to you for how long, but using that time to be proactive instead of reactive could be the difference in your energy and your decision-making.

Consider outlining your process to your team. Let them know you will get back to them and offer a time line instead of leaving them hanging. They will appreciate it and be less likely to start pushing for a response.

We discussed the art of facilitating a brainstorming session, but this may not be your cup of tea. What are you thinking when people start weighing in on the "tangent" or "interruption?" Consider the extroverted side as well. Many extroverts can't even access their own true thoughts without talking it out. You, as the leader, must figure out how to balance your desire for well-thought-out responses with those who need to utilize a group setting to bring out their best.

Many of you have bought into the idea that you must act as an extroverted leader, whether it was a conscious decision or not. The true downside for you is the exhaustion you're probably feeling. You must be careful to balance being present for your team and managing your energy. The flight attendants' warning says it best: "Should you feel the sudden decrease in pressure, an oxygen mask will drop from the overhead compartment. Secure the mask on yourself first, then help those around you."

You must pay attention to your energy level and ensure that you're recharging your personal energy battery. If you don't, the price can be high. Your business relationships, personal relationships, decision-making ability, and health are just a few of the things that will be compromised if you don't keep your energy replenished.

Consider the following strategies to make sure your energy tank is full:

- Go in early before everyone else to get a handle on the day.
- Take off a half-day during the week and work on Saturday morning when no one else is in.
- Take a walk a few times during the day, perhaps with someone you need to connect with.
- Listen to calming music through your headphones on your computer.

- Take the long way home at night to give yourself some time to decompress.

- Have staff meetings to cover information once instead of having the same conversation twelve times.

- Eat lunch alone.

- Breathe, deeply and often.

- Take regular vacations.

- Go to the gym during your lunch.

Whatever you decide to do, start now. Your attitude, health, well-being, family and company depend on you to take care of you. Isn't that reason enough?

☑**WELKnote:**

Introverted leaders understand that they need to schedule personal time to preserve and renew their energy.

Chapter 33 - Leveraging Your Extroverted Leadership Style

Extroverted leaders have an open door policy. They will often initiate the conversation, as they love to engage with other people. Since they're approachable, the idea of bouncing an idea off them is welcomed and reciprocated. Remember, they process what they're thinking by talking out loud, so they're usually looking for someone to provide feedback. This means they initiate contact and seem to spend more quality time with their teams than introverted leaders.

Typically, you will also find the extroverted leader engaging in brainstorming sessions with their teams. The process of "group thinking" facilitates the best possible outcome for their style. Often, they will engage in a conversation without necessarily picking a side and not because they have a hard time making a decision. They use the forum to hear everyone's thoughts, but mostly to hear their own. This makes the employees feel that their ideas and opinions are being valued.

All of that great collaboration, however, "your opinion matters," and "I value our conversations," could lead to inappropriate sharing of information. Sometimes people will assume what is being said is the gospel. It's too easy to take conversations out of context if you're the employee engaging with the extroverted leader. Be very careful to frame the conversations as gathering information, so as not to mislead anyone about the intent or the deliverables.

The other caution about brainstorming sessions is that they can leave out the introverted team members. The quick discussions and twists and turns are usually more fun and exciting for extroverts. What would be deemed by some a lively and productive meeting might be viewed as disorganized and chaotic to the introverts in the room. Remember, neither style is right or wrong. We are seeking to create some understanding of the dynamics needed to be mindful of when engaging your team. Honoring both styles is not easy, but it's necessary to get well-rounded feedback.

If you're extroverted, please be careful about invading the physical space of those around you. This can be annoying on its own, but add your title to the mix and it can be a liability on an entirely different level.

One of extroverted leaders' biggest regrets involves responding too quickly to emails. The down side is obvious and can be damaging to a career. If you fire back too quickly without thinking of the ramifications, the damage can be permanent. Too often emails are read out of context, as it's very difficult to know the rest of the story, and who knows what the reader was in the middle of when it was received? Timing plays a huge role in email communication and should be considered before any sensitive topics are responded to, regardless of whether you're an introvert or extrovert.

I was recently at my desk (for the thirteenth straight hour) when I received a quick response email from an extrovert on my team. He had posed a question earlier in the day that required about a dozen other people to provide input, and I was trying to connect all of the dots before I responded to him. Needless to say, his comments about no one caring about his situation did not sit well with me.

I am happy to say I deleted the first email I drafted BEFORE it was too late. I wanted to tell him all of the many variables that happened, and I wanted to bite his head off for being so snarky about it. Unfortunately, I have not been so wise in the past and still cringe remembering some of the emails I've sent to people I've offended by responding without thinking of the bigger picture. I will assume I'm not alone in that regret. Perhaps time will be kind to us for those miscues.

This is a short checklist for extroverted leaders:

- Pause before you respond to big issues (write out your email and wait one day to send it.)
- Make sure you honor the introvert's need for time and reflection on new issues.
- Don't dominate the conversation.
- Use a headset so you can stay mobile.
- Play music through your headphones to re-energize.
- Go out for lunch with others.
- Make sure you complain "up." Don't ever talk to one of your direct reports about issues you might have with those you report to.

☑WELKnote:

Extroverted leaders understand that they need to pause to make room for others in the conversation.

Chapter 34 - Temperament Theory

Many years ago at a conference, one of my clients pointed out a session she thought I should attend. She had attended the beginning of the session before lunch and thought I might find it interesting.

I walked into the ballroom at around 1:30. There were about 120 people in the room, and it seemed to be organized mass chaos. Groups of people were in break-out sessions, and large Post-It® notes adorned the walls with participants' handwriting all over them. I had no idea what they were writing, but people were truly engaged in whatever was going on.

As I looked around the room, someone from one of the groups yelled out, "Hey, you belong over here!" They seemed fun, and since it's always nice to be wanted, I immediately joined them.

I inquired about what I had missed, and they quickly caught me up. "We've divided into four groups based on the descriptions we read in this booklet. You don't even need to read it. You definitely belong with us."

I sat with them for the rest of the session, and they happened to be right. What I learned over the next few hours blew me away. The speaker, Marla Sanchez, described what I now know to be something called temperament theory. There are many different philosophers and philosophies about it, but they all lead to the same conclusion: We are born with certain predispositions toward personality development, an understanding that can greatly improve one's ability to work with others.

Here is the quick history of temperament theory. This is in NO way meant to be a comprehensive introduction:

One of the earliest philosophers, the Greek physician Hippocrates, recognized that there seemed to be four distinct personalities in his patients. He named these after the different humors of the body.

Carl Jung, a psychotherapist, concurred with the findings of four distinct personality types. He did not, however, credit the humors of the body. His theory was centered around how the brain developed.

Then there was Katharine Cook Briggs and her daughter, Isabel Briggs Myers, who were ardent students of the work of Jung. They were able to marry theory with actual data, and the Myers-Briggs personality test is still recognized today as the baseline of temperament theory.

So what does it all mean? There is very little debate about temperament theory. This research is not meant to put anyone in a box or define someone entirely, but it does give us clues about differing personalities and preferences. Understanding those differences can bridge the gap in communication in all relationships. Having that knowledge can help us be more relatable as leaders and as partners of any kind.

Attention Skeptics!

I've often watched the skeptics in different temperament study seminars. They sit politely and even smile a little, but I can see the questions in their stares. Their body language betrays them. Are you putting me in a box? Who came up with all this stuff?? Is this some kind of psychology seminar? These are just a few of the thoughts people have admitted to thinking in the beginning, and they represent many others who would not admit to their skepticism on this topic.

After reflecting on the information, bumping it up against your own experience, and paying attention to the things we discuss, you'll understand some of the mystery about how different people are. We're not trying to prove that you can figure people out entirely, but we do know that people are born with natural predispositions. Learning about those can help you get the most out of your employees and your team.

This understanding is a key part of becoming an Exceptional Leader.

As you read, reflect on your own personal situations. Be open. You'll find that some of your own personal experiences will be talked about. You'll laugh out loud at some of our examples, as you undoubtedly will have lived some of them. You will remember past relationships and wish you had known what you just learned. You will further develop your appreciation for other people's perspective and your own.

A Note From a Former Skeptic

I was more than a simple skeptic: I was an active debunker. My issues with personality and temperament identifications were not because of an aversion to psychological or sociological studies. I have a healthy respect for those disciplines and have done my fair share of study in both.

My problem with all of the various personality "types" came down to two areas of specific skepticism:

1. Can it really be productive to give people (yet) another reason to think and talk about themselves? It seemed unlikely.

2. I don't like it when things are oversimplified. To say that there are four boxes (it's ALWAYS four) that the whole world fits into seemed like wishful thinking. The effort that it takes to sell that idea seemed to guarantee that it could not possibly be true.

Then I started working with Tracy Spears. Her approach tackled the challenge of dealing with personalities from a leader's point of view and looking at it as a serious study, not just a profiling tool. The object was not simply to identify people; it was to examine and discover how to lead a disparate group of people successfully.

Tracy said, "You study this stuff so you can learn to successfully lead people who are not just like you. If someone can tell immediately what your native temperament is, you're not an evolved leader."

Checkmate. That was what I needed to hear. If studying personality types, introversion, extroversion, predispositions, and temperaments meant that I was working on myself as an evolved leader, then I was "all in." Can you succeed as a leader if you can work successfully with only 25% of the people on your team? No. How about 50%? No. A progressive leader needs to have an understanding of how people work, why people do what they do.

Every success you will have as a leader starts with your understanding of people.

- A Former Skeptic (Wally)

☑WELKnote:

Sometimes you don't know what you don't know.

Chapter 35 - Understanding the Four Temperaments

Now it's time to talk about the core needs of each personality type. After you read each overview, you should get a sense of what your natural temperament is. Remember, you're a combination of all temperaments with one being dominant.

Here are the four core needs:

1.   Relationships
2.   Duty and Responsibility
3.   Knowledge and Information
4.   Freedom

Keeping Things Simple:

In my first experience with temperament theory, I learned the four types as colors. Using colors to describe the four temperaments gives us easy terms to understand each temperament.

•   Relationships = Blue
•   Duty and Responsibility = Gold
•   Knowledge and Information = Green
•   Freedom = Orange

Let's start with the **Blue**. This is the temperament that is driven by relationships to all things. Their core need is relationships. They are the peacekeepers. They seek harmony in all situations. They tend to avoid conflict. If someone is upset with them, they will worry about it, perhaps even lose sleep over it. They have this great ability to "feel" the energy of other people or situations. They can sense when something is wrong with someone. They are ruled by their gut feelings more than the rest of us. They are very aware that we are all somehow connected. They love to be in nature. They are usually animal lovers, so not always, but often, they will have pets that have been rescued. They feel a strong need to protect all creatures.

They are the biggest cheerleaders in the group and want everyone to do well. They are true team players. They don't like winners and losers. They want everyone to be included. They usually know the names of their colleagues' children, spouse, the hobbies they have, and the food they eat. Often, they're the ones bringing food to the office for everyone. This is the temperament that can't stand it when people aren't getting along. If someone is upset with them, it affects everything they do. They seek to make sure everyone is happy. Quite simply stated, these are the self-described people pleasers.

Next, let's talk about the group that has the core need for duty and responsibility, or the **Gold**. This temperament is the most dependable. If they tell you they will do something, they will. With this group, belonging must be earned. They tend to see things as right and wrong, black and white. They are often very punctual. I'm certain someone from this temperament must be the one who invented the saying, "There's no such thing as on time. If you're not early, you're late."

They are usually very direct. They love predictable patterns. They create traditions out of events. I can ask them what they're going to do for an upcoming holiday, and they can tell me. Why? Because they did the same thing last year and the year before and the year before, etc.

This is often the list-maker of the bunch. If you're reading this and you're Gold first color, there's a high probability you have a to-do list going right now. They love the list so much that if they do something that's not on the list, they will often put it on just for the satisfaction of marking it off! They are typically the most organized of the bunch. I've seen many Gold organize the clothes in their closet by color... all white shirts together, blue shirts, etc. The hangers all face the same way, by season, by size, etc. Their cupboards are often organized by contents. All green beans are together, cans facing the front, etc. You get the picture. Also, they love the agenda. They don't like to be surprised. The Gold are all about safety, and not just their safety, but everyone else's as well. Their gas tanks rarely get to empty. Many have said they fill their tanks before they get below half. This group has a tendency to be focused on the past ... *the way we've always done it.* Often their motto is "If it ain't broke, don't fix it."

Now, on to the **Green**. Their core need is knowledge and information. They are focused on the future. Their motto might be, "If it ain't broke, break it anyway because I'm sure there's always a better way to do it." They are always thinking about how to improve a situation.

This group is all about the data. They love knowing how and why things work. They question everything and everyone. They don't care about your title or your tenure. Are you competent? Is this the best we can do? They often skip the empathy in the situation. You come in to discuss a situation or maybe make a casual comment, and they begin analyzing the situation, looking for the fix, or the essence of the story. They are trying to solve the problem and they need the information, which often leaves the other feeling interrogated.

They also spend a lot of time researching a situation so they can see all sides. Don't give them a detailed list; give them a high-level overview. Give the details to the Gold. And for crying out loud, don't send them a long, drawn-out email. Hit the high points and move on. They will ask for more info if they want it. The Green will actually have a hard time with this section because we aren't providing enough "hard" data, but once they research temperaments, we will be good to go.

Lastly, let's discuss the **Orange**. Their core need is freedom. They don't want to be tied down or boxed in. This is the group that will push the limits. Test the boundaries. If you say, "Don't cross this line," it's merely an invitation to see what will happen when they do.

They love a challenge. They are highly mobile. They are very kinesthetic. They are fluid, great at going with the flow, but if they want to go a different direction, they will. They don't like the agenda or the details. Rules will bog the Orange down. They are usually entertaining and always have some adventurous story to tell you. They are the best in crisis. They see natural short cuts, and they're very resilient.

They are also the most competitive of all of the temperaments. They compete about things the rest of us don't even know are going on. Can they make it through the traffic light before it changes from yellow to red? Can they be the first ones out of the parking lot after the concert? Can they pick the right line at the bank drive in? If you ever ride in their car, you'll notice the car never quite comes to a stop. They hate the idea of sitting still in traffic and will travel 10 miles to go 5 if they can take the highway and avoid the traffic lights. They will cut through the parking lot to avoid stopping as well.

The Orange are the most generous of the temperaments. They will give you the shirt off their back ... literally. They might come back and ask for it in a few weeks when they realize they need it, but they weren't thinking about that in the moment they gave it to you. They live in the present. Consequences? They will deal with those later. Here is the thing to remember about Orange: The more freedom they have, the less freedom they need. Don't micro-manage this group. Give them the outcome you're looking for and let them figure out the how-to.

With this information, which temperament sounds the most like you? Which one sounds least like you? If you had to put them in order of most like you to least like you, what would your order be? Are you Gold-Blue-Green-Orange, or Blue-Orange-Green-Gold?

Let's look at a few different examples:

1. Someone whose color order is first Blue and last Green. This person is intuitively able to connect to the emotions of the situation. They are aware and often guided by how people are feeling about the situation at hand. Their decisions will take the feelings of everyone that is affected into consideration. This is a gift of someone that is first color blue, but sometimes they're held hostage by the feelings of the people on their team. They will hesitate to make changes that will upset their team.

2. Someone who is first Green and last Blue. They will look at that same situation from a more data-driven point of view. They will connect to the business side of the situation first and make a decision based on facts, not feelings. They will often be accused of not caring about people, which isn't necessarily true. They do care, but they will not let that determine their final decision. Everyone might be upset, but they will come to realize it was necessary to make the changes.

3. Someone who is first Gold and last Orange. This person will want structured and well-thought-out plans and will be frustrated by people who "wing it" or want to stray from the tried and true methods. The opposite person will view the structure and planning as too rigid.

It's important to know how this all plays into understanding the people you lead. Often people will ask, "What is the perfect color order?" The answer is simple. The best order is someone who is equally developed in all because the order can determine the point of view of the leaders. Remember, we are not putting anyone in a box; nor are we suggesting you're one-dimensional. We are helping you understand why people do what they do and how you as a leader can influence them. Having a better understanding will make you more able to work effectively with each of the temperaments and allow you to get the best out of everyone on your team, something all exceptional leaders know how to do.

☑WELKnote:

Temperament Fluency gives leaders an understanding and appreciation of the gifts and perspectives of the people they serve.

Chapter 36 - How Temperament Fluency Makes You a More Effective Leader

Have you ever hired someone who just "got" you, someone that you've never had an issue with or any kind of misunderstanding? That person knew what you liked, what you didn't like, and what you expected. He or she just seemed a perfect fit from the very beginning.

No? Me neither.

If you come upon any situation, ten people will tell ten different stories about what happened. They have different perspectives. They have ten different lenses from which they're viewing it. Our job is to figure out which lenses our people are using so we can be more relatable as leaders.

The leadership style that says "my way or the highway" has limited success. That type of authority does little to encourage teamwork, loyalty, and creativity. It does even less to move an organization forward in the way that a collaborative community does. The autocrat has a short productive lifespan with a team, especially a high-performance team.

What about leaders who make all their decisions by consensus? They're afraid to upset someone or leave someone out, so they spend a lot of time and energy accommodating everyone on their team, only to realize it's impossible to please everyone. There's a lot to learn about collaboration and consensus-building. Many experts now say that the best ideas are typically defeated in a collaborative setting. It's worth studying.

Before you read about how to connect with each temperament, take a moment and write down two or three people you find it difficult to work with. Think about how you interact with them and why this interaction seems difficult for both of you. Perhaps that list can help provide context for this section.

Connecting with the Blue Temperament

Let's start with the Blue, whose core need is relationships. If you listed a Blue as someone you struggle with, it could be because this person will be most driven by feelings. Remember those big feelings are also their gift. Blues are the best at bringing warmth, unity, and camaraderie to a team. It's important that you provide the more empathetic side of the company and of yourself. Blues will usually ask more personal questions in attempt to create a connection.

When you introduce a new policy or procedure, Blues will be in tune with how everyone feels about it. It goes without saying some leaders couldn't care less about how everyone feels when there's a company to run. I get that, but you should care. Turnover and unhappy employees cost too much for any organization.

Most importantly, these employees have the hardest time separating who they are from what they do. If you criticize their work, they will probably feel that you have criticized them. I've watched leaders avoid coaching these gifted employees because they didn't want to hurt their feelings. I've also seen them be discounted because they're afraid they will get overly emotional or because they don't stay as objective as other temperaments. While that may or may not be true, it should not diminish the importance of providing them necessary feedback. Instead of avoiding the tough conversations with them because you don't want the drama, figure out how to lead them to a more logical point of view. Connect them to the bigger picture. This group can serve as the emotional compass for a company. They make people feel that they're part of something special. No spreadsheet can do that.

Connecting with Gold Temperament

Gold is driven by duty and responsibility. This is the person who loves the rules, structure, and yes, the agenda. While the Promoter Leader might be more concerned about how everyone feels, the team members are concerned about everyone doing what they're supposed to. Belonging must be earned with this temperament. You aren't doing your job? You should be warned, then fired if you don't straighten up. You're ten minutes late? Unacceptable. Confrontation? Not a problem for them. They don't mind being the ones to tell you the truth–as they see it.

These are also the historians of the company. What have we traditionally done? They have the answer. They like to talk about the way it used to be. They are the best at telling the tribal stories and reminding everyone how far the company has come. They provide much-needed stability and standardization to any organization.

Connecting with Green Temperament

Someone who does like change? The Green Temperament. There's always a better way to do it, and these leaders love trying to figure that out. We've always done it that way? That's actually the best reason to do it differently. They like the big picture. Give the details to Gold; give the bottom line to Green. Holding unnecessary meetings or saying the same thing over and over is likely to drive them mad. They need information from you, but they like gathering it on their own as well.

They will sit at the table of their very first staff meeting and start asking, "Why do we do it that way?" They will question everything. Gathering information along the way will help them think about how to improve the process. It will feel like they're questioning your authority. They are. Why shouldn't they? Just because you're in charge is no reason you shouldn't be challenged. They assume you have a well-thought-out reason for everything, and sharing with them is part of your job.

This is the group that skips the empathy in the conversation. No need to worry about their feelings because they aren't being guided by them anyway. The data is the thing. Feelings are too subjective and solving problems is more fun.

Connecting with Orange Temperament

Lastly, let's talk about the Orange. This is the temperament that needs freedom, freedom from the agenda, from the details, the structure, and the mundane. To get the gifts of this temperament, you will need to buckle your seat belt and hang on. They are very present and focused. Your timelines and agendas that make you feel safe? They simply annoy this group. The more you try to box them in, the more rebellious they will be. The key to working with them is very simple. The more freedom they have, the less they need. Give them outcomes and drop-dead deliverables. Let them come to you with their questions instead of trying to tell them the best way to do it. Your way will only serve as a challenge to do it differently. They will see and take shortcuts naturally. Let them. They perform well in a crisis and will not let everyone get bogged down with the details.

Try to provide deadlines for them. They don't want your structure, but they probably need it. Your job is to figure out how little or how much. Want to coach them? Do it informally. Make suggestions that will lead them to the desired outcome. Challenge them. They love contests and winning … and having fun in the process of accomplishing their goals.

Important Comment

The bottom line is that you're not leading colors: You're leading people. We are merely using different terms to help you connect to the different needs of each temperament. Knowing their core needs can help you understand how best to interact with them.

The strategies for each temperament add up to one strategy that makes us all better leaders. Incorporate a sense of value for all of the temperaments in your day-to-day leadership. If you were to honor every temperament in your company, it would look like this:

- Value the people and the process.
- Provide structure and value the standards that have gotten you here so far.
- Provide vision and let people be part of making things better.
- Have a fun atmosphere that values individuality and is not rigid.

Who wouldn't want to work for this kind of leader? Remember, it's your job to incorporate the gift each temperament brings to your company. Being able to marry those gifts with the company objectives is one of the cornerstones of Exceptional Leadership.

☑WELKnote:

Temperament fluency gives leaders the ability to understand what motivates each person they serve

Chapter 37 - Developing Leadership Temperament Fluency

Once leaders have identified the core need for each team member, they then understand the different approaches needed to get the most out of those they serve. In the beginning, it will feel mechanical to change your approach for each person. It can even be exhausting, as it is with any new skill.

It's worth noting that you're probably already connecting very well with a good percentage of your team, as you certainly share the same temperament with some. We're talking about growing your ability to influence *all* of the people you serve in your leadership role. We want to flip the way you view those that are difficult to connect with from, "I just can't work with him because of how he is," to understanding that it's not because of who he is, it's because of who *you're not* as a leader. This means 100% accountability. No more "my way or the highway," or "because I'm the boss" for you. You're ready to be an Exceptional Leader!

Can you imagine the capability of a leader who has learned how all of the temperaments are wired and how to work best with each of them? A leader who knows how, when, and what approach to take in different situations to elicit the best possible outcome with every employee? That is leadership temperament competency.

One of the best ways to understand how expertise actually develops is through the classic competency ladder described as the "Four Stages of Learning Any New Skill" by Noel Burch in the early 1970s. The next step for the truly exceptional leader is to develop an "unconsciously competent" level of understanding of how to work with each temperament.

Let's do a quick review of the stages, and then apply them to how a leader would become an expert in her understanding of temperaments.

Stage 1: Unconsciously Incompetent = I don't know that I don't know.

Stage 2: Consciously Incompetent = I now know that I don't know.

Stage 3: Consciously Competent = I know, but it takes a lot of concentration.

Stage 4: Unconsciously Competent = I automatically know, and it is second nature.

Do you remember what it was like the first time you rode a bike? Before you were even aware bikes existed, you were at stage one. You were unconsciously incompetent. You had no idea about bikes or your lack of ability to ride one. The moment you sat on the bike and attempted to ride it, you entered stage two. You became consciously incompetent (and *screaming* for training wheels ... or was that just me?). Stage two is tough for people because you realize you're not any good at something. Most people try to avoid this stage because it is uncomfortable not knowing how to execute something. This is where fear really gets and keeps most people from even attempting new things.

Back to the bike. With a little bit of time and practice, you finally hit stage three, where you were consciously competent. You knew how to ride, and you could ride without the training wheels, but you really had to think about it. You were riding the bike with a fake smile and white knuckling the handlebars! No multi-tasking at this stage. Lastly, you hit stage four, which is unconsciously competent. You could ride without any assistance or thought. You jumped on your bike and rode without thinking about your balance or falling.

We are all at stage four with many things that happen every day. Breathing, walking, talking, driving (unfortunately), and perhaps even in how we treat people.

Just to make sure you're distinguishing the stages of competency, take a minute to think of one personal example you have in each of the four stages. You will find it hardest to think of a personal example in the unconsciously incompetent category. This is because these are topics, skills, and knowledge outside of your current awareness.

Look at the competency ladder with details of temperament competency added in.

Leadership Temperament Competency Chart

	No Awareness	Learning Fluency	Fluent	Effortlessly Fluent
	Stage 1	Stage 2	Stage 3	Stage 4
Blue Leader (Promoter)	You never consider how things are affecting the people in your organization.	You know people are unhappy, and you're uncomfortable or avoid them.	You realize people need your time and attention, and you engage them instead of waiting to be engaged.	You don't worry about how you will navigate emotional conversations. You value people for who they are and what they do.
Gold Leader (Planner)	You have no idea people are seeking structure and rules.	People are asking for more accountability. Perhaps policies and procedures need to be more clearly defined. You're aware and taking on the task is daunting.	You provide job descriptions, objectives, deliverables, and agendas. Everyone is clear about the expectations, but have to be reminded.	You're a well-oiled machine. All T's are crossed and I's dotted. You're prepared, and so is your company. Everyone has accepted the policies and integrated them.
Gren Leader (Ponderer)	You seem aloof to your team and engage only in high-level conversations.	You know you need to make an effort to connect with your team, but it takes a lot of energy, and you aren't sure of the payoff.	You're responsive to people who need details and interaction. You provide it because you know it will lead to getting the best possible outcome.	You're able to value the input from your team, and the emotional outbursts are not interpreted as character flaws.
Orange Leader (Performer)	Everyone around you is stressed and needing direction.	You attempt structure, but it feels like someone is boxing you in.	You embrace the rules and regulations needed to create a more productive environment.	You have systems in place and have created a more predictable environment. You're not always in a Chinese fire drill, but not bored either.

What did you select as your color order? Remember, you're born with a combination of all temperaments, but one is dominant. You develop the others over time with experience. Your 2nd-4th order might even change, but your first color will always be first. Knowing this, what do you see in the chart above about your own competency? Are you unconsciously competent in all areas, or do you see an opportunity to develop?

Statistically, there's a higher chance we will have a conflict with someone whose first color is our last. That makes sense. People who have our same first color share some of the same foundational thinking. For example, Golds need structure and like rules, so when someone else suggests a template or policy change for something, Golds are already in agreement about the need and now just work through how to get it implemented. Suppose there's an Orange sitting in the same meeting. The last thing they want is structure and rules. They are looking for more freedom and FEWER rules in most situations. Thus the conflict begins. Everyone probably wants the same outcome, but the methods to get there will be different.

The next time you're in a meeting and someone says or does something that you cannot connect with, consider their possible temperament. Are they just being true to their core needs? What is the core need they're trying to fulfill? How does that employee react when you empathize with them instead of ignoring or discounting (intentionally or unintentionally) their point of view? What does that do to the culture of your company when you start saying, "Help me understand" instead of not engaging them?

☑WELKnote:

The steps for learning temperament fluency are the same as for learning anything else. It is a study and requires awareness, commitment, and practice.

Chapter 38 - Your Temperament Strengths & Blind Spots as a Leader

The last section introduced temperament theory, defined its purpose, and helped you understand what your people need from you. Now it's time to go deeper.

How does your innate temperament affect your team? Celebrate the gifts that make you an effective leader, but also look for your potential blind spots as well.

Considerations to keep in mind:

1. Many "problem" relationships we've had in the past make a lot more sense when viewed through temperament theory.

2. Fluency in understanding temperaments is just like learning a new language.

3. That colors that describe your team will not be sufficient descriptors for moving to the leadership level

We can build a bridge from the simple "colors" descriptions to how they manifest themselves in leaders. Once you attain a level of temperament fluency, you will see people and leaders around you very differently. What were once confusing motives will become clear. The fog will lift on what were previously inexplicable personality conflicts.

Here are the temperaments, along with a Leadership descriptor to make each easier to grasp:

Blue = Promoter Leader

Gold = Planner Leader

Green = Ponderer Leader

Orange = Performer Leader

The Promoter Leader (Blue)

Let's take a close look at Promoter Leaders. We've talked a lot about how supportive, caring, empathetic, and nurturing this temperament is, but the truth is those amazing qualities can also create issues for this leadership style.

These leaders have a tendency to avoid confrontation. Their need to have everyone like them can make it difficult for them to acknowledge poor performance. It's difficult for this leader to have a tough correcting conversation without worrying about hurting someone's feelings. Other temperaments will be able to keep this separated more easily, but for the Blue Leader, the relationship is part of all conversations.

The Promoter Leader will also make exceptions for their employees to keep people from being upset. They will let things slide, and small things may result in a giant volcano. When they finally do blow, it seems out of proportion to the situation. People are often caught off guard because there's no warning that anything is wrong.

It seems to come out of the "blue," and rightly so. You're always positive. Always cheerleading everyone. You want everyone to like you. You almost choke on the words you want to say, but don't so you can keep peace and harmony in the workplace. Meanwhile, your employees are being lulled into a rhythm that indicates all is well with you. They are oblivious to the fact that you want to strangle them.

Consider having the conversation *before* it gets that far. Believe it or not, people really do want the truth. They want to be coached. They deserve to be told what the expectations are and given feedback before it's too late. It's a setup to do it any other way. No one wins when either party is holding back any kind of communication about the job at hand.

Lastly, be mindful of having "off the record" conversations. You're the most approachable leader, which is good and bad. People will feel like they can ask you or tell you anything, which will occasionally lead you to conversations that you probably shouldn't engage in. Learn how to redirect and give non-answers. If you're upset about something, make sure you complain "up" and never, ever engage someone on your team in a negative conversation. What you say has a much bigger echo because of your title.

The Planner Leader (Gold)

Now on to the Planner Leader. Their leadership motto is "Belonging must be earned." This leader is great at providing structure and feedback for their staff–maybe a little too good. They are quick to point out faults and offer suggestions for poor performance. The two questions this leader should consider are:

1. Is my way really the only way to do it?
2. How much structure is the right amount for each person on my team?

Planner Leaders have a tendency to micro-manage their employees. While it's true the structure serves as a blueprint, it can also serve as a straightjacket for some. They're often known as the traditionalists of the company. They like doing things the way they've always been done. This also means they have the most difficult time with change. I'm not saying they can't change, but that it's more difficult for them than the other temperaments because they can get bogged down in the minutiae of things. Their need to be able to manage the risk will sometimes be an impediment to pulling the trigger.

If you're Gold, remember that new ideas can bring risk to an organization, but can also bring great rewards. Try attending a meeting and thinking about the possibilities people are talking about instead of just looking for ways to poke holes in the ideas being discussed. Being able to avoid risk for the company makes you valuable, but it just might keep you from the change needed to make sure the company is viable in the future.

The Ponderer Leader (Green)

Speaking of future, let's talk about the Ponderer Leader. Change? Bring it on. New ideas? I'm on board. That's the way we've always done it? That's a good reason to do it differently. This does sound like a great type of leadership and it is, but it has its liabilities as well.

These are the leaders who love a challenge. Bring them a problem, and they'll fix it. What we love most about Green leaders is that they're trying to make us better. They always think about how we can improve. Who doesn't want that?

It turns out that more than a few people don't. It's not the new ideas you provide that bother people. It's the lack of detailed explanation about the "new" direction you're trying to take your team. What seems obvious to you can be challenging to others. You might not need the details and "what ifs" answered, but for those who do, your ideas can be frustrating and hard to connect.

Remember, these are the conceptual leaders. Details bog down creativity and serve as impediments to progress for the Ponderer Leaders. Can't people think for themselves? Why do I have to tell them every single detail of this?

If anyone is out of control emotionally, these leaders will actually begin to question that person's credibility. They tend to view emotional people as "soft." The danger in this is obvious.

Remember the saying by Zig Ziglar: "People don't care how much you know until they know how much you care." It's very difficult to get the most out of your employees if you never connect with them.

If you're a Green, know this. Not everyone gets it. It doesn't mean they won't; it just means you might have to lead them through the process. Also, remember people are involved in the processes you're trying to change.

The Performer Leader (Orange)

Do you know how to find out if you might be a Performer Leader? Well, for starters, you probably skipped everything before this to get to your type of leadership. HA! You're impatient. You're the fun leader. You love a good debate. You will negotiate anything. You love contests, and you love to win. You love shortcuts and enjoy giving options to your employees. No micro-managing with you, no sir. You generously give everyone the freedom that you so desperately want for yourself.

Oh. No one is doing what they're supposed to? That could mean they might need a bit more direction than you're supplying. The thing your team loves about you is also the thing they complain about. The freedom is fun for a while, but at some point it's just plain chaos. They need to know what you expect. They need a job description. Deliverables. Structure, even if it's just a little bit.

Though this type of leadership is fun and exciting, it's very hard to perform if you're not an Orange employee. The motto for the Orange is ready, fire, aim. Though it's exciting, it can also be terrifying for others. Your fun spirit can be unpredictable. Your last-minute deadline when they need to leave on time for a family function is irritating. And though your constant need to change is exhilarating, it's also impossible to predict. The mid-stream changes create a lack of confidence among your team.

Here's the truth: Though you value freedom as an Orange leader, it's well known that you need structure. Find a way to create accountability for you and for your team. Have conversations about their job descriptions. Give them feedback and direction.

One final caution for the Performer Leader: Stay connected to the people you report to. One of the biggest challenges for this temperament is that they will be viewed as so easy going and maybe not ambitious. That could not be further from the truth. Be the life of the party, but make sure you remind people of your value to the organization and of your work goals.

Let's end this section with something that should be obvious, but needs to be said. I don't care what your color is. I don't care if you're hung up on which style best describes you or not. We discussed some distinct strategies that, without the colors, are solid strategies for all leaders to adopt.

Just to be clear, they are:

1. **Tell people the truth.** *Have* the difficult conversations. You cannot effectively lead people if you're always concerned with being popular. You must be the truth-teller, even when it's hard, even if someone doesn't like you.

2. **Think outside the box.** Look at everything with fresh eyes. Don't let inertia set in on your leadership. Be open to new ways of seeing things, and don't let the rules trump common sense. Be skeptical of processes that have been the same for too long.

3. **Connect with your team.** Always staying in your head leaves little room for relating to your team. How are you showing them that they're your top priority? That connection is what will create undying devotion from people.

4. **Make sure you're having some fun.** We spend as much or more time at work than we do with our families. If you're driving into the parking lot dreading the day, your team is too.

Which of the four are you really good at? Where could you use some work? Take a minute to write out the ideas.

☑WELKnote:

Exceptional leaders understand that their greatest conflicts and challenges typically come from people whose dominant temperaments are their own least-developed temperaments.

Exceptional Leaders Know that Leadership = Influence

Chapter 39 - Developing Personal Influence as a Leader

A multitude of books, blogs, and articles have been written over the years about how to gain influence as a leader. *The Art of War*, written by Sun Tzu well over 2000 years ago and generally regarded as the first leadership book ever written, is focused on this subject. Thousands of leadership books later, how to develop influence as a leader is still a topic worth studying.

When we think about developing influence as leaders, we all come to the idea with a different motive. What is it that we want to influence? Is it other people? Is it strategy? Is it culture? Is it our own careers or reputations we are trying to influence? It's safe to say that all of these motives fall into the category of ambition. We want to gain influence because we're ambitious, and that is usually a very good thing.

The *Harvard Business Review* published a study focused on how managers choose subjects for professional development. The study, authored by Amy Cuddy, Mathew Kohut, and John Neffinger, shows that managers and leaders tend to choose training programs and literature focused on technical competence over the "soft skills" of management and leadership. The managers in the study overwhelmingly believed that they would become better leaders by becoming better at certain skills. The great majority of the managers in the study were strongly focused on technical and business skills instead of personal traits like warmth, trust, understanding, communication skills, and likeability.

The authors point out that putting competence first actually undermines leadership influence. To quote the article: "Without a foundation of trust, people in the organization may comply outwardly with a leader's wishes, but they're much less likely to conform privately–to adopt the values, culture, and mission of the organization in a sincere and lasting way."

The study demonstrates that, in the pursuit of influence, most leaders are far too focused on techniques and short-term learning. They believe that they will grow their influence by adding certain technical or tactical skills. Developed leaders understand that there's much more to gaining, growing, and leveraging influence than just broadening your skill set.

Growing Your Influence by Raising Your Hand

One of the best ways to grow your influence and importance in any organization is to take on projects. In every company, branch, or division, there are a few people who have developed a reputation as volunteers. These people are usually no more experienced or skilled than their peers, but they have the spirit and confidence to raise their hands when they have an opportunity to be involved with something they think is important.

The results of this consistent involvement can be amazing. These people make connections all over their organizations and develop new and valuable skills. In addition, these adventurous volunteers end up on the top of everyone's list when it comes time to start something new or organize a new team.

Do you raise your hand when you see an opportunity to do or learn something new? Do you reach out to other groups or departments when you see a chance to make a positive impact? Most people actively avoid additional projects that are outside of their main job descriptions. Don't let that be you. Raise your hand and gain new skills, new perspectives, and a new reputation for involvement.

Get Out of the Consensus Business

As managers and leaders, we have people who report to us and people we report to. Most of us also have some de facto peers. These are people distributed across our companies, departments, or divisions who are at our same level ... whether they have our same title or job description or not. When you work in peer groups, one of the strongest negative forces is the tyranny of consensus, or decision making by majority. Building a consensus within a group on a certain topic seems like a positive, even a democratic thing, doesn't it? So why is the pull of the majority view a negative force?

Habitually working towards consensus has a way of taking passion and personal advocacy out of decisions. We have all been there: You're discussing a topic in a group, and everyone is weighing in. By the time everyone has added his two cents, the dynamic nature of a conversation always begins to leak energy. Even groups of very smart leaders tend to make decisions that are simply the average of everyone's opinion. The power and motive force of advocacy falls away when the consensus view is adopted. This is especially true in creative fields like design, programming, branding, sales, marketing, and advertising.

When you're trying to grow your influence, you have to change some of your behaviors. Getting out of the consensus business is one way to influence the groupthink malaise that many organizations have engendered without even knowing it. When you're working with your peers, and you're working on something that you really care about, make your voice a voice of advocacy. If you do not have a strong opinion on a topic, there's no reason to involve yourself in the decision. You would only be contributing to the average of the opinions, and when decisions are made using the average of the opinions (AKA the consensus), nothing dynamic or interesting ever happens. You will grow your influence by understanding that decisions should go where the passion and advocacy is, not towards the majority or average of all the opinions.

Growing Influence by Developing Protégés

This may be the most positive way to grow your influence in your organization. When a leader makes it her business to help other people grow and develop their skills, they're planting seeds that will sprout and grow in ways that leader never could have imagined. You have certain understandings and perspectives that you have learned with time and experience. These perspectives and specialties are your currency for positively influencing people who will need to know these things to improve in their roles.

The goal for every leader should be to:

1. Develop real skills that can be leveraged to improve people and teams.
2. Make sure that these skills are consistently demonstrated and taught to new and aspiring leaders so that the effects of these skills and perspectives are multiplied.

Developing protégés inside and outside of your area of responsibility has a tremendous ripple effect for them and for you. Some highly influential leaders have dozens of protégés they have mentored through their careers, and most will never even use the words *mentor* or *protégé* to describe the amazing effect they're having with the people they get to work with. If you want to grow your influence, focusing on growing other leaders is a great place to start.

Myths About Growing Influence

There are many myths about growing influence. Most of these have to do with personality, office politics, and leadership styles. Probably the biggest myth is that you can grow your influence by ingratiating yourself to people above you on the organizational chart. This strategy is not effective for two reasons: (1) Trying to be liked and respected by your superiors will do nothing for your credibility with your team, and (2) most modern organizations are in constant flux and the brown-nosing strategy won't hold up if you try it again and again with successive bosses.

Here are some other common myths about growing influence:

- You will grow your influence by trying to sound smart and using the latest business clichés.

- Being critical of other people is an effective way to grow your influence in your group.

- You will grow your influence by disassociating yourself from people or projects that seem to be failing.

- Being the 'funny guy' or the biggest personality in the group is a great way to grow your influence.

- You can grow your influence by changing companies often; being the new person gives you extra credibility.

- It's easy to grow your influence by taking credit for other people's work or their ideas.

Of course, none of these ways of attempting to develop your influence will work. Remember, we aren't trying to grow our influence temporarily or increase the appearance of influence. Real and permanent influence comes from actual skill, successful results, and measurable impact.

Thermostats and Thermometers

Think about the difference between a thermometer and a thermostat. Most of your peers and most managers everywhere are thermometers. They can tell you what the temperature is. They understand the environment they're in.

Influential leaders are thermostats. They *set* the temperature and they can change the environment when they need to. These leaders are the ones who influence their organizations, day in and day out. It's as simple as this: Be a thermostat, not a thermometer.

☑WELKnote:

To put it as simply as possible, effective leadership is the ability to influence people toward a common objective.

Chapter 40 - (En) Lightning Leadership

I love the double entendre of this chapter title. Okay, I cheated on the spelling, but I had to in order to make the point. One image is a lightning bolt leader who demands you take notice, while the other takes a more subtle, more effective approach that isn't always as obvious, especially to those who aren't paying close enough attention.

First, the lightning bolt. I'm sure you've had the experience of hearing or experiencing something that practically sent electricity through your body. Someone said or did something, and you remember where you were and what you were doing when it happened. Depending on your age and where you live, you probably just thought about the Boston marathon bombing, the shooting at Columbine, the tragedy at Sandy Hook, or maybe even the day Kennedy was shot.

But have you ever had the lightning bolt moment that wasn't attached to a tragedy, yet still changed you to your core? Maybe it was through a conversation, a glance, or a comment at just the right time. Maybe someone said something or did something for you that changed how you thought about things. Who has given you that jolt at just the right time, when you needed someone to believe in you so much that it pulled you through a dark or challenging time?

Here's a better question: Whom have *you* done that for? Have you delivered some important jolts?

It takes an enlightened leader to realize how much influence he can have over his people, to really understand how important his or her role is in the development of who someone becomes.

Merriam-Webster defines *enlightened* as: "Having or showing a good understanding of how people should be treated; not ignorant or narrow in thinking." I love that. It's an explanation that isn't trying to manipulate people into performing or acting like the bottom line is all that matters. Being enlightened simply means the treatment of people is a priority, along with the profitability of the company. These leaders have the ability to rise above the petty issues of day-to-day management and connect to something much bigger. They remember that "who people are" and "what they do for a living" are connected in important ways.

Being an enlightened leader means you're aware. You're aware of the need to be careful with your title and your power. You're the leader who remembers the golden rule of reciprocity, who recognizes the value of the people *and* the profits. Isn't that the person we would all run through walls for? I know I would.

☑WELKnote:

Exceptional Leaders have the ability to provide a "jolt" to their people in the right way at the right time.

Chapter 41 - The Amazing Power of Trust

One of the important distinctions between a manager and a leader has to do with the responsibilities of their jobs. Most managers are expected to keep things moving, avoid accidents and blow-ups, and keep their hands on the wheel. They have targets and issues to resolve, and they can have a ton of responsibility. Leaders, on the other hand, are expected to improve things, grow the business, or possibly even take it in a new direction entirely. When you're a manager, you expect people to do their jobs the best they can. When you're a leader, you expect people to do things they have never done before.

Because of these distinctions, leaders who expect to take their teams from one performance level to another must be prepared for certain kinds of exposure. A leader who expects her team to perform at a very high level has to expect some disappointment, some conflict, some challenges, and some significant setbacks. These are all part of the job for people who want to lead high-performance teams. Leadership is hard and requires that the leader will go "all in" in the pursuit of extraordinary results. One attribute trumps all others when it comes to laying the foundation for significant success and growth in a team environment: trust.

To talk about leadership without talking about trust would be like talking about a TV without mentioning the screen. Trust, or the lack of it, is the most visible part of a leader. No matter what a leader says or seems to value, the existence of trust will be apparent to everyone around him. Does the leader talk about the value of the team and then strategically bet against them? Does the leader talk about the capability of a certain group while clearly devoting more attention, more money, and more resources to another group?

There are three aspects of trust that we, as leaders, all need to understand and develop:

1. Trust in ourselves
2. Trust in our people
3. Trust in the process of growth

Trust is one of the most powerful and least understood creative forces in influencing organizational excellence.

Developing Trust in Ourselves

You, the leader, are the foundation of all of the success or failure that will occur in your area of responsibility. This being true, we must be able to trust our own intuitive ability to make decisions and trust both the long-term and short-term outcomes of these decisions. Often the people above us in our organizations will judge our effectiveness by the short-term effects of our decisions. In contrast, the people below us will make their judgments based on the long-term results and how these results will affect them personally.

This presents a challenge, especially for the middle manager, and clearly sits opposed to the true health of your business, district, department, region or division. It looks like "talk about the mission but fixate on the quarter" is going to be the model for the majority of organizations for the foreseeable future. This is a shame, because this contradictory way of measuring progress is certainly responsible for turning at least one generation of would-be leaders into a bunch of role-players and cynics. The upside? This does present an opportunity for a smart and progressive leader like you.

Because of the "you can't please everyone" reality of business, a responsible and well-intentioned leader must satisfy her own principals and priorities first. This is where the self-trust comes in. Do you trust your own vision enough to follow a strategy that may not be exactly what the folks above and below you may be expecting? Are you willing to work through some ups and downs in the pursuit of an exciting long-term objective?

We have two choices as leaders developing our identities in our organizations:

1. Be the yes-person for the people one or two layers above you by always saying the right things, adding to the consensus, and saluting the right ideas.

2. Be a popular leader for your own team and advocate for it while being sensitive to the team's concerns and priorities.

The long-term undesirability of both of those choices is clear. You have examples of both kinds of leaders in your organization, and it's easy to tell who's who. The independent and progressive leader must learn to find his own way. That means taking actions that you believe (trust) will take you where you want to go and ignoring the short-term reactions of the people around you.

Along the way, you'll be developing a reputation as someone who can single-mindedly focus on a result and ignore the noise around you. This is a much more valuable reputation than either of the variations listed above, and you will actually get important things done.

So if we're going to chart our own course, how do we make adjustments to avoid risk along the way? By long-term observation and experimentation. There are basically two methods of making decisions and adjustments along the way in any leadership initiative. They are the same two ways that you learned long ago: proactive and reactive learning.

Our real goal is to have the ability to learn and flex in our plans and actions as leaders. Any ambitious professional knows that consistently poor decision-making can put even the most conservative plan at risk, but if we're going to try to accomplish extraordinary things, we're going to have to do things differently with ourselves and with our teams.

Reactive Learning

This method is also known as "trial by fire" and "learning from our mistakes." You really don't have a choice in this one; It's just going to happen throughout your career. The real benefit of experience in a certain role is that you get to put some of these kinds of lessons behind you. Of course, reactive learning is very useful, and it has the obvious advantage that you can "reactively" learn good lessons from other people's bad decisions. We have all watched a really bad idea or execution forever alter someone's reputation or career path.

You have probably worked with so-called leaders who learn all of their leadership lessons in this piggy-back kind of way. They take no risks at all and seem never to act on their own ideas. The biggest drawback to learning exclusively in this reactive way is that you will acquire basically the same lessons, skills, and competencies as anyone else who is working in the same environment. Because of this, learning in a reactive way rarely leads to breakthrough implementations or ideas.

Proactive Learning

My understanding of the overused and under-defined word *proactive* is that of "an idea- based decision or action." Applying that definition to leadership learning leads us to think of a person who can act on instinct *and* follow through on plans. This leader can execute ideas while accumulating lessons on wins and losses, which will gradually form a foundation of valuable experiences that will serve you well. They will build your professional skill set, your credibility, and keep your creative juices flowing. Even the "failures" will be valuable in another situation or context.

Progressive leadership experts have always told us that to improve we must fail frequently and that most ideas become "good" or "bad" based on their timing or execution. Ideas sometimes need to mature and take form under different circumstances to succeed. The proactive learner tries many ideas and avoids marrying any of them, all the while carefully evaluating outcomes for future use. Today's innovative leader cannot afford to have his whole identity or reputation tied to one idea, one area of passion, or one theme. Nothing is more important to your future as a leader than having a long list of (possibly) great ideas awaiting their time.

High-potential leaders are simply leaders interested in aggressively learning and then generating ideas. The people we call thought leaders put a much higher priority on observation and sensitivity than they do on office politics and leadership posturing. We should all aspire to be leaders who are more into being "interested" than being "interesting."

This all feeds into the over-arching idea of trusting yourself as a leader, trusting your instincts, trusting your ability to learn on the fly, and trusting your decisions. The decision to answer to your own strategic vision even when it's not popular is an overt act of self-trust. Your personal credibility is at stake, and your team will know it. This is an important moment for any leader.

☑WELKnote:

Effective leaders understand that trust is something they earn over time, and without it their possibilities will be drastically limited.

Chapter 42 - Developing Trust in Your Team

The next crucial area for leaders to develop is trust in their people. This may be the area of the greatest contrast between leaders: how they choose to view their teams. A significant percentage of people in leadership and management roles believe that their current team's limitations are to blame for performance shortfalls. Many of these leaders have basically postponed the accomplishment of anything meaningful until they have "the right people." I constantly talk with otherwise capable managers who really believe that there's a certain person or combination of people he will eventually "find" that will put his organization in the record books forever. They believe that high-performance teams are built on a foundation of innate talent and chemistry rather than on development and expectations.

This is a deadly belief for a leader. Not only is it profoundly incorrect, but it's also fundamentally lazy. A leader who blames poor or average results on his team is the worst kind of leader. Why? Because this leader is not only insulting the people he's supposed to be leading, but also excusing himself from the responsibility he has a leader. Progressive leaders know that they're responsible for *developing* a team of standout people capable of extraordinary results.

There is a broad distribution of talent, ambition, intelligence, intention, background, and motivation in a business environment. Every group of individuals is a mixed bag of many, many different attributes, strengths, and weaknesses. Effective leaders have the ability to look at a group in terms of its upside. These leaders understand that individuals are basically smart and ambitious and would rather succeed than fail ... period. If those beliefs resonate with you, then you have a great team of hardworking, committed people. If the description sounds naïve, then I'd be willing to bet that you have staff problems that you think will be solved when you find some of the "right people."

Don't worry if this is you; you may have good reasons to be a little cynical about your team. That said, there's no way for a cynical leader to drive extraordinary results. If your general feeling about your team is negative, it's worth your time to think about why you feel this way.

Leaders might feel negative about their teams because:

- The team was assigned to you, and you had no real choice in the personnel.
- The team is comprised of former peers who may not completely support you.
- The team has a history of poor or average results.
- The team is not diverse. They all seem to be good and bad at the same things.
- The members of your team have been in their roles too long.
- You just don't like most of them.

There are numerous reasons why leaders might be a little down on their teams, but be mindful of the statement above: There's no way for a cynical leader to drive extraordinary results. Something has to change for you to take your team in a positive direction. How do turn your people into the "right people"?

The first thing to understand is that your team is always a reflection of you. This is true whether you like it or not, and the longer you have worked with a certain group, the more true it is. Fact: Our real beliefs and expectations about our people will dictate our relationships with them and influence their desire to contribute.

Ask yourself:

- What are your general beliefs about the people on your team?
- Do you believe that every one of them has the capability to succeed and contribute?
- Do you know what their goals are?
- Do you believe that your team is strengthened by its level of diversity?
- Considered individually, are your people in the right roles?
- Does your team really understand what you're trying to accomplish together?
- Is it obvious to everyone how they personally benefit from the team's success?
- Is everyone's role on your team clear?

These can be tough questions when they're answered honestly. It's important to understand that your desire and ability to be honest with yourself regarding your core beliefs in these areas will set the speed of your progress as a leader. Really thinking through these questions will help you get a handle on the idea of "finding" vs. "developing" people to contribute to your organization. Clearly, some people are more able to succeed in certain job situations than others. It should be obvious to all of us that talent, intellect, experience, expectations, motivation, and preparation will have a great deal to do with a person's likelihood of making a big impact in an organization.

That being said, we must also be open to the fact that these factors mostly exist (or don't exist) independent of active leadership. It would be a mistake to invest too much of our leadership interest in isolating these attributes alone. We would be better off concentrating our attention and skill on areas that will allow us to differentiate our organization or team from all of the other talented, experienced, motivated, and prepared teams.

As leaders we need to concentrate on providing the best situation for a person to succeed in. We need to think creatively about what makes a work situation valuable to the individual who is in it. We need to keep our minds open to new ways to engage our teams and embrace their individual motivations.

Here is an example of a perception change that really worked for me when I was leading a sales team. About ten years into my management career, I became aware of a very simple idea that helped me accelerate my team-development confidence and ability. This concept allowed me almost immediately to be more responsive to the people who wanted to succeed in their positions.

Here it is: *I work for my people's goals*. It's almost too simple, isn't it? As a leader, I make sure everyone knows his responsibility and opportunity. Then I make certain that I understand their individual ambitions and motives, and then I go to work *with them* towards their goals. When the individuals on my team succeed, the collective results can be surprising and amazing.

As simple as this idea is, it is the very definition of mentoring and is clearly more reliable for making meaningful progress than any management "style" or strategy I have studied. This concept succeeds even when it fails. Here is what I mean: If the person in question won't work diligently towards his own goals, he certainly will never work towards yours. This incontrovertible truth can help a leader be more decisive in getting rid of non-contributors. If a person in your group will not even work passionately toward his own supposed goals, he will never work towards any organizational objective. The implication of "working for people's goals" is formidable and requires a great deal of leadership trust.

If you commit to working towards organizational objectives from the direction of your people's goals and ambitions first, you can expect to be rewarded with both quality production and meaningful progress over the long term.

☑WELKnote:

An Exceptional Leader will do whatever it takes to build and demonstrate trust in his or her people.

Chapter 43 - The True Cost of Conference Calls

"Let's schedule a conference call each week to go over the sales pipeline for our team." Seems logical. Seems like something we should all be paying attention to, so I put it in my calendar for the entire year at 8:30 Central time for every Wednesday morning.

We always start promptly at 8:30 and usually end in an hour. I get to hear the other VPs cover their pipeline, and they get to hear mine. In the beginning, this was really needed. I needed the accountability, and I enjoyed learning from the other VPs. The dialog was thought provoking, and I enjoyed connecting with my counterparts. We landed many of those early prospects and solved issues around the client experience for our customer. All of this had been very beneficial, to say the least.

Fast forward two years. We've been having that same call every Wednesday for 104 straight weeks. We may have skipped a few, so let's call it 100 weeks.

Depending on which website you use, we work on average 1,500 hours a year, though that number seems like a part-time job to me. Let's use it to make the point.

If you earn:

- $50,000, your hourly income is approximately $33.00 per hour.
- $100,000 = $ 66.00 per hour
- $150,000 = $100.00 per hour
- $200,000 = $133.00 per hour
- $250,000 = $166.00 per hour

What is that conference call costing me and my company each year? Let's say all six VPs make $150K per year. $100.00 per hour X six VPs X 50 weeks we are on the call = $30,000 per year. Multiply that by the two years we've been on each week, and the company cost has been $60,000 so far.

That's right, $60,000 to be on a call each week for one hour. We all know that would never be approved as a budget line item, and it is a cost that goes unquestioned in many organizations.

Now, I'm not in favor of canceling all conference calls. Some are necessary to the business, but the real question is this: How many calls are you requiring your team to be on per week that might not be necessary? This example is only one hour per week. My guess is many of you are having two, three, four, five or more calls per week that are costing more than they're earning. What if you said you could easily cancel two standing calls per week? On our team, that would generate over $100,000 per year in savings.

But let's go deeper. What could your team do with that extra time each week? What if you asked them to talk to your top customers during that same hour for the next 52 weeks? How about if you asked them to call a top performer for your company? Or mentor someone who is an up-and-coming producer in your company? Or take an online course? How much business do you think those calls would generate? What about the "opportunity cost" of the other things these leaders could be doing during these calls?

Because we don't write an hourly check each day to our team, it's easy to lose sight of the value of their time. Rethink your automatic conference calls. Look at the things that need more attention and have a bigger upside than a bunch of suits sitting on a call, waiting for their turn to talk. Create accountability utilizing different methods other than the dreaded conference call. Finally, remember to calculate your own hourly fee and make sure you're getting the most out of your day as well.

The bottom line here? Be very wary of events and activities that are recurring or automatic. Those calls or meetings seem to take on their own momentum, which can take precedence over other more important things. For the next thirty days, ask yourself, "Is this call/meeting even necessary any more?" You won't rid yourself of all the predetermined calls, but canceling a few of those will probably yield you the few extra hours you need to catch up on other things. If you're really lucky, maybe you'll be able to enjoy a weekend or two without worrying about what isn't getting finished. Okay, that may be a stretch, but I hope you get the point.

☑WELKnote:

Pay special attention to anything in your business that seems to run on its own momentum. Often, the usefulness of an idea or event runs out long before it's actually ended.

Chapter 44 - They Are Not Here For The Money

If you could poll employees at various companies about what really motivates them about their jobs, you would be surprised to find that most people are not money motivated. There's a lot for leaders to learn about lining up rewards and recognition with employee temperament (and a little common sense), but the payoff will yield more productivity, loyalty, and job satisfaction than any 3% raise ever has.

We have all been in that no-win conversation with people about their "worthiness" of a raise. People have written books on how to get up the courage to ask for the raise, what to say, what not to say, and how to say it to get a "yes." I'm all for people deserving more money; the problem is that for most, the raise completely misses the point. The most important thing about getting a raise is what it truly says about the person receiving it. It signifies that someone is valuable to the organization. They matter, and what they do is actually making a difference.

I would argue that few people are passionate about their actual jobs. What they're usually passionate about is the people they work with or the difference their job makes. In my day job, I work for a collection and billing company. You might think that sounds like watching paint dry, yet I work with some of the most passionate people I have ever met. The passion stems from the service delivering amazing results for the clients and for the other people who are selling that service. Our company meetings are usually 20% about the product and 80% about the people. No one gets choked up talking about the new collection of auto dialer technology (though it's exciting), but watch someone introduce his or her team, and you will see true passion.

When you get a group of people together who appreciate each other's contributions and feel that they're somehow making the company better, you have the culture that most companies can only dream about. That kind of culture does not happen without a few people infusing and maintaining great leadership along the way. It takes an ability to combine the needs of the company and the needs of the people in a balanced and sustainable way.

So how do you show people they matter and exhibit your appreciation for what they do? Here are just a few examples of different ways leaders show appreciation for their teams:

- Flex time
- A few extra days off
- Individual recognition (such as birthdays and work anniversaries)
- Mentoring programs
- Creative time
- Appointment to committees
- Hand-written notes
- Team building meetings
- Brainstorming sessions about the future of the company or department
- Incentive gifts
- Movie tickets
- One-on-one time with you
- Giving additional responsibility
- A book with a note in it
- Casual day, Hawaiian shirt day, sports jersey day

If you can't offer anything on the list, just saying "thank you" can go a long way. We could write a book about this, but the take away is clear.

People want to feel important. If you really want to know what you could do to show your appreciation, ask them. I promise you will get your best ideas from the people you're leading. Ask them how you could show your appreciation. You could do it in an open forum or ask them to submit their ideas privately. Better yet, what are some of the ways you would like to be appreciated? That might be a good starting point!

And about that raise? That would probably be okay too.

☑WELKnote:

Exceptional leaders understand the transformative power of appreciation and recognition.

Chapter 45 - Trusting the Growth Process

Leaders have to learn to trust themselves to lead and know the different ways to build and sustain a positive trust in their team members. Now we come to the big picture, developing an abiding trust in the process of growth.

Most of us have had the experience as leaders where all of the pieces seem to be in place, but the performance of the team is still lagging behind our expectations. We also know that no truly high-performance team ever reached that status without many setbacks and disappointments. Most experts on highly productive teams and groups agree that these periods of underperformance are actually necessary and should be considered part of the process of developing an exceptional team.

Over my twenty-plus years of leading teams, the words "trust the process" have become my mantra during inexplicably difficult times, such as when the effort and the results did not seem to match up or when the results lagged far behind the expectations. "Trusting the process" means having the confidence and faith to hold your expectations high for your team and all of the observers. There can be no hedging. When a project or initiative is wavering and the leader appears to be less committed to the outcome, things can spiral downward quickly.

This is most visible in sports, where you can actually observe the players of a losing team watching their coach to see if he's concerned about how things are going. If the coach sends signals of weakness (berating players, changing strategy, weak body language) the players will begin to "play smaller," which is usually the first step towards giving up. When the coach appears to have faith in the plan and maybe even seems more confident in the eventual outcome, the players will clearly begin "playing big" and doing the things they know the coach/leader expects them to do. Watching team sports with these thoughts in mind is like seeing a leadership clinic every weekend. Teams rise or fall to the leader's expectations.

Most skilled leaders have learned to exhibit this counter-intuitive confidence when things are moving slowly. They do and say things to demonstrate even more faith in their team when things are going poorly. To these leaders, the outcome is a foregone conclusion because of the three kinds of trust, trust in themselves, trust in their teams, and trust in the process of growth. They will overcompensate with confidence and overt, visible trust.

Leading people is an amazingly complex process, and the results cannot always be measured quantitatively. In fact, you could say that if most of your perceived progress is of the quantitative variety (in the numbers, rather than in the culture), then your real leap forward is probably quite a ways off. We must understand that in every enterprise or project there will be necessary periods of disappointment. Leaders who can see these periods as the raw material for growth have truly learned to "trust the process." They put the short-term failures into an understandable context for their teams and allow them confidence to do the work that will lead to success.

Trusting leaders learn to look for these meaningful short-term failures. High-performance teams grow in a five-steps-forward and two-steps-back rhythm. Paying attention to and recognizing the necessity of small failures and disappointments is one of the best ways we have as leaders to demonstrate our confidence in our people and our plans.

☑WELKnote:

Smart leaders recognize setbacks as a necessary part of growth. They know how to plan for and manage through those situations ... leading their teams to greater success.

Chapter 46 - Leadership vs. Manipulation

Before we dig into this topic, let's all agree that there's a place for manipulation in business, and there are times when teams and organizations must be manipulated to get them to a certain place. The idea of manipulation is not, in itself, negative. It's a necessary skill and tactic, but it's grossly overused in many organizations. Why has it been overused?

Because manipulation is easy. It requires no homework or even an in-depth understanding of the people being affected. Like any easy thing, it's done too much. This is especially true in big organizations.

The line has been seriously blurred between leading and manipulating. These synonyms and descriptions help us see the clear contrasts between the two:

Leading = Influencing

Manipulating = Persuading

Leading = Developing

Manipulating = Directing

Leaders think: I believe in you.

Manipulators think: I believe I can use you.

Leaders think: How can we lead them?

Manipulators think: How can we make them?

Leaders say: Let's do this together.

Manipulators say: Do this for me.

Leadership: Long-term gains

Manipulation: Short-term gains

Leadership: Hard

Manipulation: Easy

Why is so much of leadership actually just simple manipulation? It's just so easy to do. The truth is that only developed leaders really understand the difference between the two, but leaders who employ manipulation routinely really believe they're leading.

This is one of the least-understood reasons why many executives have such short periods of real effectiveness with new teams: They never learned how to lead. They really believe that the manipulative interventions they're executing represent some kind of active leadership. Their intentions are not necessarily bad; they're just not fully developed leaders. Of course, we all know that just shaking things up does not make people better, does not make customers happier, does not build a brand, and does not make businesses more valuable.

There's a time for both, but we need to recognize when we are manipulating and when we are leading. Here are a few common examples of each. None of these tactics or strategies are necessarily good or bad, but it is important for developed leaders to be deliberate with their choices and not fall into the habit of using manipulation routinely as so many ineffective leaders do.

Manipulation Tactics:

Reorganizations

Contests

Reassignments

Territory changes

Successive short-term promotions

Management threats

Leadership changes

Switching performance incentives

Leadership Tactics:

Training

Shared accountability

Performance coaching

Focused campaigns

Coaching

Long-term strategies

Participative decision-making

Leadership development

Most of us work for companies clearly using one set of tactics or another, either manipulation or leadership. A few of us are in situations where we see a lot of both, and these are usually organizations where most people report to more than one boss.

One of the most frequent observations we make in working with companies where the leaders have over-manipulated their teams, is that the people tend to be quite cynical. It's almost as though they have become enthusiasm-proof. You can almost see "What now?" written across their faces. This is what the use of manipulative tactics does to an organization over time. Passion and enthusiasm are replaced with cynicism and a jaded approach to change.

Manipulative tactics always appear in high-pressure environments. The more job security pressure or investor pressure there is, the more short-term oriented the management becomes. Things can get really confusing here for even the best leaders. Many will default under pressure to using manipulative techniques, even if they know the results will only influence the short-term.

What kind of leader are you? Have you overused manipulative techniques? Think about it. As a developed leader, you don't want to always do what is easy and expedient. You want to do what works. We are not in business to have a great month or quarter, so why would we employ short-term manipulative techniques that will gradually blunt our credibility and effectiveness over the long term?

Developed leaders know how to pick their spots and leverage situations. They employ occasional short-term tactics overlaid on a clear path of tangible and expected improvement. They are coaches who would never risk their biggest leadership asset, their credibility, for a temporary gain. Take some time to think through your approach.

☑WELKnote:

Exceptional Leaders know how to use many different strategies to drive results. They understand that different situations call for varying approaches.

Chapter 47 - Creating A Place For People To Contribute

You've worked hard for years to be finally promoted, or maybe you're a young up-and-comer that people are noticing. Regardless, you have some authority and you're ready to use it! But things are not going exactly the way you imagined they would. You had an idea of how your team would respond to your leadership, and this is not it. What? Not everyone is listening to you? They aren't doing it "your way"? They are actually pushing back?

You're now ready for the truth about real leadership. I'm not talking about being the boss. I'm talking about genuine leadership. Being a great leader has very little to do with who you are or how you came to be the boss. As Zig Ziglar famously said, "It's not how much you know, it's how much you care."

I don't take that to mean the "touchy-feely" type of caring; what I'm talking about is a gut level understanding of where your people are coming from. What makes them tick? What struggles are they facing in their job? What keeps them up at night? Do you know why they show up every day? Is it because they need the money? I doubt it. Is it because you have provided an amazing vision they want to be part of? I hope so. It doesn't matter to your team one bit how smart you are, how much you know, how long you've been in your job, or even your title. What really matters is simply ... do you inspire them to want to be better?

You may say, "I thought being the boss meant we would do things the way I wanted them to be done. After all, isn't that the point?" The truth is that being a leader can be the most pride-swallowing, tongue-biting, gut-wrenching title there is. Having authority just means you have a greater responsibility to understand the needs and wants of the people on your team.

I love a good debate. I actually get nervous when everyone agrees with what the "leader" is saying. My first thought when everyone agrees is, "Have we seen this from all sides?" Most people don't understand the value that dissent brings to a situation. They feel it's antagonistic or slows the group down. Sometimes it can be, but having a diverse group of people brainstorming is the best way to assure you have looked at all sides of the situation. Also, if your point of view is 100% solid, polite dissent will give you an opportunity to further explain your position and earn more buy-in from the team.

- I've even seen leaders fire people who didn't agree with them. This can be the worst thing a good leader can do. I shudder to think of the people who have been promoted because they agree with everything the boss says. And I mean everything!

- Here are two direct quotes about people who were promoted in a company I have worked with. They got the job because they're "easier to manage" and "they won't create waves." I am all for a team that gels together, but the truth is the people with differing opinions represent the only effective way to expand your current views as a leader. Think about it. We never change our minds without taking in new information. To provide all angles, you need people on your team who are not "yes people".

Have you surrounded yourself with "yes people"? Do you have anyone pushing back on your ideas? Have people quit raising their hands? Are they quiet on calls? Maybe a better question is, "have you shut down someone because you couldn't manage the feedback?" Is there someone who used to have a lot to say and is now quiet?

An inexperienced leader will feel threatened by dissent. I speak about this from experience. A case in point: I hired a lady about eight years ago. She came into my office one day inquiring about why we were using a particular script. I answered with the tried and true response. I said, "We've always used it and have gotten good results." She walked out of my office and went to every single person on her way back to her desk and asked them what they were using as well. Of course, the answer was the same: "the one we were told to use." One of my business partners came in my office, shut my door, stood with her hands on her hips and said, "I can't believe she's questioning everything! That girl's not going to make it!" I smiled, appreciating the "support" and thought, "Of course she's not."

I needed to address that clear lack of respect (an undeveloped leader's view), so I went to her desk and made her a deal. "If you think it could be better, why don't you bring me your thoughts and let's agree to use either my script or yours. Fair enough?" She agreed. Of course, I knew the outcome. She would realize that "my way" was the "best way" and come in apologizing for even questioning me.

So I waited. In she came. She seemed excited. How odd. I assumed she would start apologizing and explaining how after many iterations, the script was really fine the way it was. She did not.

She handed me the new script. I read it. I re-read it. I read it again. I wanted to tear it apart, tell her why mine was better, and explain how someone who had been in the business for a few weeks couldn't possibly make a change to something better than what we were using. After all, I had been with this company for fifteen years. I'm the authority, aren't I?

Well, I couldn't. Her script was flawless. It spoke to our target audience. It articulated our offer. It was short and to the point. It presented a compelling concept. It asked for the appointment. It was exactly what we should all be using.

In that moment, I realized I had not kept up with the times. I was stuck in "That's the way we've always done it." I had not questioned that script once in the fifteen years I had been using it. Why would I? It was still yielding good results. It still set appointments. I loved how comfortable I was training it.

I'm happy to say that in this case, I was smart enough to swallow my ego and tell her the truth. We don't have space here for me to tell you about how many times I did not have such good insight. She was right. Her way made more sense and sounded better. Perhaps the timing was good. Maybe the hundreds of books I've read on leadership were taking hold because I was actually grateful she brought a new perspective to something I considered to be tried and true.

I always associated great leadership with structure, rules, and regulations. Those are a big part of leadership, but they should never define it. Great leadership should include a foundation for people to thrive, but should also include innovation, flexibility, freedom, connecting, change, experimentation, and fun.

Most importantly, great leadership needs to create a space for other people to contribute, a place where all strengths can be honored and valued, regardless of who generates the ideas.

☑WELKnote:

Sometimes the most effective thing a leader can do is just get out of the way and let people produce.

Chapter 48 -The Problem with Motivational Leadership

A myth permeates many of today's business organizations, a myth played out in many businesses, but especially in situations requiring a high level of energy and activity from the workers. These might be start-ups, network marketing groups, and sales organizations. This myth has to do with the worker's motivations, and where they actually originate. This myth can be at the root of debilitating arrogance in many managers and supervisors in relation to their teams.

Put simply, the myth is that "management" is somehow responsible for the daily motivation of the people they work with. This conclusion has been sold to all of us as a leadership skill in this way: If a manager or leader is a good "motivator," the team will produce more and generally outperform a team whose manager has been less successful in motivating the team. This idea's weaknesses are obvious to anyone who has ever been subjected to an insensitive or unskilled leader's force-fed motivation. It's a practice especially transparent to X- and Y-generation workers, who are particularly internally-driven and sensitive to manipulation.

The motivational leadership conceit has existed as long as there have been bosses, but it seems more prevalent these days. The whole idea of "motivate" as a verb should be questioned by any serious student of leadership. A thoughtful leader will see that it can be an arrogant or insensitive way to lead people. This is mostly because any leader who is mainly focused on motivational leadership is probably making two incorrect assumptions:

1. That the workers themselves do not have enough self-motivation to want to work successfully.

2. That individual performance is best influenced from the outside, by some action, decision, or manipulation by a manager or leader. This might be a motivational speech, a contest, a new corporate theme, or new mission statement. Anything that is meant to influence team performance without any additional training, coaching, or resources.

Is there a time and a place for old-school motivational leadership? Of course. Our challenge, in trying to be exceptional leaders, is to make this kind of leadership situational and make it the exception to our normal coaching.

People have their own motives and reasons for working. It's certainly true that some motives make them more valuable to the company than others. It's okay to admit that there are people coming to work just to collect a paycheck with the least possible work or involvement.

On a high-performance team, these people present a real risk. That does not make you cynical. What is cynical is to believe that—without the benefit of a leader's motivational assistance—the majority of your team (or company) would not do their best or worse, that they would do as little as possible to stay on the payroll.

The traditional motivational model is lazy. It has not changed substantially since the 1950s. It rose up from the sales and network marketing culture and made it all the way into the buttoned-up offices and boardrooms of corporate America. It can still be seen in the motivational posters we have in our halls, in the slogans we use to fire up the troops. Motivational platitudes can be heard in the voices of our most inspirational leaders. If you listened closely, you could hear an ironic echo in these messages that made you doubt their sincerity, but they still exist today.

Isn't it time to admit that these types of hackneyed, shorthand, get-some-boost-without-actually-training-new-skills tactics are a type of manipulation? Would you like to estimate the number of meetings, seminars, and conferences that were complete wastes of time and money because of this approach to "motivation"?

Sales managers and sales executives are the guiltiest by far. I know because that's where I come from, and I've been guilty of trying to get real results from this kind of lazy leadership. There is a huge industry built around sales managers' insatiable appetites for the newest motivational fuel for their teams. If today's managers were as hungry for new coaching techniques as they were for new motivational ideas, we would have a lot more successful teams. That seems obvious, doesn't it?

So why are we so attached to this idea of motivation? When we have collectively become so much smarter about compensation, key business measurements, successful selling behavior, helpful technologies, and better learning tools, why do we still cling to four-generations-old ideas about how to help our people perform better? Here's why:

1. **Low career risk.** These ideas about motivation allow managers and leaders to "lead" with very little accountability. If their motivational techniques seem to succeed, then all glory (and credit) goes to them. They successfully sparked the team, at least for the short term. Conversely, if the manager's team does not respond to her motivational efforts, it's very easy to blame them instead of her. How many times have you heard a manager talk down about his people because they did not sufficiently respond to his fiery speech? In these situations, the manager has no accountability to the outcome, just the glory if it works and the right to be critical of his people if it doesn't. It's an attractive win-win situation for the manager.

2. **It's cheap.** Real training, coaching, and skill-improvement initiatives are expensive. They require talented trainers who really

know the day-to-day business challenges (which many executive-level managers do not). Real training demands real preparation and forethought. Traditional motivational techniques can be executed without this level of planning and can usually be delivered with comparatively little expense.

3. **It's scalable.** You can do a motivational speech or seminar in front of 10 or 10,000 people and basically say or do the same things. Sometimes having larger groups can even make the event seem more substantial. Traditional one-way motivating is a broadcast. You don't have to know the individuals or even the collective needs or challenges of the group. You don't need to worry about actual skill gaps that might exist in your people. You only need to motivate.

4. **It's ego gratifying.** What is more stimulating to a leader's self-image than the idea of standing behind a podium or speaking through a webcast and inspiring the team? Many leaders really like to hear themselves talk. They like to hear others talk about them. We became business leaders, not rock stars or professional athletes. Delivering this kind of motivational message gives us our chance at that kind of attention, maybe even a standing ovation.

5. **It's all we know.** Many of us grew up in business with this kind of leadership as our examples. Motivational leadership was what we thought real leadership actually was.

6. **It appears to work sometimes.** Occasionally a motivational event can really arouse people. It can be magical and make people feel the way they feel with powerful music or an inspiring film. We have all experienced this kind of inspiration. We've been so pumped up that we wanted to kick down the doors of the conference room as we left. The question remains, however; are people actually going to be better and more productive? Or are they just really excited?

The most useful starting point is to consider what you're really trying to do. Are you looking for actual business improvements? Is the goal to have an outcome that you can measure? If so, then you should consider how to go about the process of improving your team. There's certainly a place for motivation leadership, but it must be used sparingly and with a specific short-term purpose in mind.

Everyone has motives. Everyone, including you and me, has reasons for the things we do and don't do. The very best way to help people improve is to get out of the motivation business and begin the real work of learning how to find the motives that are already in your people. Once you understand and catalyze the motives of the people you're leading, you increase performance in permanent ways.

Short-term motivation has a place, but it's not going to yield sustainable progress or real growth for your people. Real business results only from doing the hard work of discovering the motives of your people (why they come to work, what they hope to accomplish, what they hope to become) and starting to work on shaping opportunities around those motives. When people have the skills and freedom to do their best, they generally will.

☑WELKnote:

Exceptional Leaders know that sustainable growth comes only from developing people through focused coaching and the investment of time and attention.

Chapter 49 - Tell The Truth

There was an abrupt dismissal of a key executive recently in a company that we consult with. He was the CFO, a trusted and tenured part of the team, and a high-profile person and well-known by many people in a large corporation. The company president made the announcement in a conference call with the executive team in this way: "Effective immediately, Joe CFO is no longer with (the corporation). We are interviewing replacements and you will all be apprised when we make a hiring decision. Does anyone have any questions?"

Sometimes executive decision-making is so questionable that there can be no questions. A message delivered in this way has wide-reaching consequences. The president, not realizing the cost of a hasty (and clumsy) communication, was not aware of the following repercussions:

- He was the one who had built up the former CFO's influence and credibility with the rest of the management team. When he tries this again with the replacement CFO, he will sense the skepticism that he caused with his abrupt termination of the replacement's predecessor.

- Other important people in the company become very aware of their dispensability as a result of the president's cavalier handling of a major change in the executive team. Will they start looking for a more secure place? Will thoughts of self-preservation affect their productivity?

- Using the phrase "effective immediately" sounds very harsh and certainly calls into question the departing CFO's credibility. If a firing is with cause, it should be noted. If not, then insinuations should not be made with careless language. This is especially true when the departed has been a valuable part of the team. It's possible to upgrade a position without downgrading the previous person.

In situations like this, the word *careless* is the most appropriate description of how the communication of personnel changes was made–without care for the departing person's reputation, the feelings and insecurities of the rest of the team, or the manager's own reputation and trustworthiness. Changes happen. People lose their jobs, but forethought and good judgment become all the more important when leaders deal with the negative inevitabilities of business.

The Truth About Truth

One of the disorienting things about the current business environment is how easy it is to impress people with honesty. Employees, peers, customers … everybody is impressed when someone is simply and plainly honest. Honesty is even referred to as a "strategy" in some contemporary business writing. The upshot is this: People who are honest by nature are finally at a real advantage. Telling the truth when it's not easy or when it sets you back in the short term demonstrates a strength of character now considered rare.

The phrase "telling the truth" itself is very compelling because "knowing" the truth seems easy, with all of our data and automated report. Still, this ability to *tell* the truth has been made to seem perilous in many modern business environments, especially when that truth impedes today's profits or questions what the numbers say.

Some companies follow policies that directly contradict their mission statements or which preach customer centricity when their actual business strategies demonstrate that customer service is a non-priority. There are even businesses that preach a "people first" philosophy while actively marginalizing them.

People with the ability and integrity to speak up about the reality of a situation or condition are key to improving a business. There's a certain gravitas attached to a clear-eyed truth teller in any group, even when that person is relatively new to the team. We would never recommend critique and provocation as a career strategy, but we would suggest that becoming known as a person who can consistently discern and communicate the truth in key situations is a very valuable person in today's business world. When you think about your personal brand and reputation, think about the personal and career value of being a reliably honest person.

☑WELKnote:

Being an absolute "truth teller" should be a non-negotiable part of an exceptional leader's character.

The Exceptional Leader's Personal Reboot

Chapter 50 – Why A Leader Needs A Personal Reboot

Think about what happens when you reboot your computer. Everything goes dark for a few moments, that strange buzzing sound stops, and when it comes back alive all of the background programs have been shut down and the computer is waiting for you to initiate some action. You're looking at a machine that is refreshed and ready to work.

If only it were this easy for leaders!

It's not, of course. A real leadership reboot should be taken seriously. It requires planning, preparation, provisions, and scheduling. Most of us cannot take a one- or two-month sabbatical and, let's face it, most of us are not good at shutting down our "work brains" anyway. So let's focus on what we can do, not what we can't.

Real leaders are engaged, paying attention, and plugged in to everything going on. This kind of engagement has its own risks and worries. We are going to make some very specific recommendations in this section, maybe even more specific than you would expect or ask for. The specificity is mandated by this truth: Sometimes a leader needs a re-boot.

What can we do?

- We can understand the need for occasional periods of mental and physical refreshment.

- We can see how the forces of habit and routine can become dangerously powerful for leaders who are not paying attention.

- We can focus our efforts on certain activities for a finite period of time.
- Even before we start this kind of regimen, we can discern how a little new discipline introduced into our lives can do a lot of good.
- We can appreciate how planting new mental seeds will eventually yield new ideas and decisions.

The Exceptional Leaders' Personal Reboot is a series of priorities and activities designed to put leaders back in touch with their most creative, most engaged, most dynamic, and most energized selves. The Reboot is designed to help individual leaders attain an optimal mental and physical state for exceptional leadership.

Let's start with our provisions. You probably already have most of the things on this list. We promise that anything you will need to buy on this list will be well worth the small investment. You will need:

✓ A fresh notebook and binder

✓ An MP3 player

✓ Good walking shoes

✓ Index cards of different colors

✓ A timer

✓ Herbal tea and/or good coffee

✓ The Seven Habits of Highly Effective People Audio Book–Steven Covey

✓ Pens and a highlighter

✓ Weather-appropriate active wear

✓ An understanding partner or spouse

✓ A strong desire to get out of autopilot mode in your professional life

Get these items organized before you start. Then we will describe the step in the following sections. Most of the really important thinking comes right at the start. Ready? Here we go!

☑WELKnote:

Sometimes "right now" is the best time to get started.

Chapter 51 - Your Energy Audit

Sit down in a quiet place with your notebook, pen, highlighter, and index cards. Think through what a weekday looks like for you. Start from the moment you wake up. Write down in your notebook every routine act you have through the day. This is not your "to do" list; this is a list of the consistent things you do throughout the whole work day. Do the same thing with a typical weekend day. List the routines you normally go through on a Saturday or Sunday or whichever days are your non-work days.

You should have two lists in front of you. Now take your highlighter and highlight everything that is optional on both lists. These are the tasks, routines, and actions that you're currently doing that you could quit doing if you wanted to. Do not highlight anything that you do not consider optional in your work and non-work routines, like taking the kids to school or attending staff meetings at work. These lists should be of things you have been deciding to do routinely.

Next, take out the index cards and make a stack with two different colors. Go back to your list of optional habits and routines and answer a simple question for each: "Does this routine add energy or take energy from me?"

Use one color of the index cards for the routines that add energy and put a plus sign on each. Use another color for those habits that cost you energy or enthusiasm. Of course these will get a minus sign. Take your stacks and set them aside.

☑WELKnote:

Knowing and understanding where you are spending your energy will allow any leader to preserve that energy for the most important parts of their lives.

Chapter 52 - Your Areas of Neglect Review

Everyone has areas that should be getting more attention. This is especially true for busy leaders like you. It's impossible to be at the top of your game in every single aspect of your life, and no one has ever done it. A neglect review sounds as exciting as a root canal, but it's actually an area full of exciting upside for most of us.

Get up early one day with your coffee or tea and sit in a comfortable chair. Take your notebook and think about the areas of your life that are not getting enough attention. These are areas that might have been a big priority for you at one point in your life, but have slipped into the background.

Typical areas of neglect are:

- Physical fitness
- Love and attention being paid to partners/spouses
- Education and self-improvement
- Special time being spent with a child or parent
- Creative endeavors like painting or gardening
- Recreational activities like tennis, bowling, or golf
- Your spiritual practice
- Involvement in a charity or cause that you care about

You will be able to identify one or two areas that will become immediately clear for you, perhaps something you had already been thinking about. Remember, these are areas of opportunity in your life. We all have them, and thinking about spending more time and energy on them is a purely positive exercise.

Once you have identified one or two areas of neglect, write them on one of your index cards. Along with the noted area, add a short description of the benefit that would come from paying more attention to the area(s) of your life you have neglected.

☑WELKnote:

Honest self-reflection can be the catalyst for making important changes.

Chapter 53 - The 3 in 6 Goal Setting Technique

This is a short, but crucial part of your Reboot. We developed the "3 in 6 Goals Setting Technique" because we work on our goals in a tightly structured way to get right to the important stuff. This is a remix of a few proven formats used by many top experts on goal setting, and it absolutely works. This process we will describe immediately separate wishes and daydreams from goals.

The "3 in 6" comes from the condensed nature of the technique. We will take exactly six minutes to go through three crucial steps. You will need your notebook, a highlighter, your timer, and six minutes of quiet time. Ready?

Step One

Write down every goal you can think of in the five goal categories:

- Things you want to DO
- Things you want to BE
- Things you want to HAVE
- What you want to EARN
- What you want to GIVE

You will write as many goals as you can in three minutes. You will get stuck a few times and those prompts—Do, Be, Have, Earn, and Give—will help you think of other goals. Set your timer for three minutes and begin.

Step Two

Now we introduce a time element to your list. Next to each goal you listed you will write a 1, 3, 5, or 10+. This is the estimated amount of time it would take to accomplish each goal listed.

Is it a one-year goal? Will it take three years? Five years? Will a few of your goals take ten or more years to accomplish? Set your timer for two minutes and think through your time estimate for each of your listed goals, writing the corresponding number next to each.

Step Three

This is the final step, and it's hard. We will limit the number of goals you have in any single time category. Experts understand that by limiting the number of goals, you actually increase the probability of reaching them. Think about it: You're not going to accomplish goal number eight if you can't accomplish goal one, right?

Here are the rules: Each of your goals already has an associated time category. You're allowed only three goals in any of those time frames, so you will select three and eliminate the rest. You get a maximum of three goals in each time category. It's no fun crossing out goals, but by doing so, you move yourself closer to the most important ones.

You will have more goals in certain time categories. Some people have far more short-term goals and others have more long-term goals, harking back to the temperaments we studied previously. It doesn't matter how many you have in any category; you keep only three. Set your timer for one minute and identify the top three in each of the time categories.

Congratulations! You finished the three steps to the optimized "3 in 6" technique. You now have a list of twelve (or fewer) goals that have been filtered by time and importance. You have joined an elite group of people who look at their life priorities in this sophisticated way. The best part? That list of goals just became one of your most valuable assets.

Before we move past this step in the Thirty-Day Reboot, we want to encourage you to teach your teams, spouses, partners, and kids this process. You will have some of the most interesting conversations with people and learn about aspirations you had no idea about, maybe even from your spouse.

☑WELKnote:

The most successful leaders start with goals and go confidently forward from there.

Chapter 54 - Revitalizing Your Mind & Body

Now you have organized some really important aspects of your life in new ways. You have your list of optional routines and habits dissected into two categories, energy-giving and energy-taking. You have one or two areas of neglect where you would like to put more of your time and energy. Finally, you have your list of goals organized into time categories and prioritized. Those of you who are participating fully in this Reboot are feeling some optimism and momentum by now.

Now let's put that work away for a while in a folder or binder. We'll return to it later.

Here is where you'll need your walking shoes, weather-appropriate clothes, and an assist from Mr. Covey. Here is the recommendation: Over the next week, start your day with a brisk walk listening to Covey's *The Seven Habits of Highly Effective People* audio book.

No one has ever distilled the characteristics of successful people and exceptional leaders better than Steven Covey. The content sets up nicely for a one-week regimen with one habit per day. Trust us on this one; your mind will be at once cleared and refreshed with these amazing lessons on character, time, self-improvement, relationships, and ambition. It does not matter how many times you have read this book, you will hear things that will click for you and help you see aspects of your life differently. Each section is less than thirty minutes, so it makes for a nice walk, too!

Leadership Wellness *by Barclay Schraff*

Working at peak effectiveness as a leader cannot happen when your mind and body are not working together. We have enlisted the help of an expert to help with some specific recommendations.

Barclay Schraff is the Corporate Health Coach at the Wellness Council of Arizona and owner of Elemental Wellness Coaching. She's uniquely qualified to give us some recommendations to help our bodies keep up with our revitalized minds.

Let's review Barclay's specific recommendations for increasing your overall wellness:

Wellness, as a term, gets tossed around a lot these days. But what does it really mean? According to the National Wellness Institute, *Wellness is an active process through which people become aware of, and make choices toward, a more successful existence.* I like this definition because it reminds us that we are each responsible for our own success. No one can do it for us. We have to want to take a close look at ourselves and then accept the self-knowledge that results.

Next, we commit to making changes and envision how these look moving forward. It's an "active" and ongoing process, with no one formula that works for everyone. Each of us has unique challenges, yet wellness is available to all of us who actively participate in the journey.

Tracy and Wally have done a great job of outlining a Personal Reboot that fits our definition of optimal wellness. The Energy Audit and Neglect Review boost our awareness of what's working and what's not. The Managed Goals Workshop is where we make the choices that propel us toward personal success.

For many of you, the Energy Audit and Neglect Review revealed potential health-related areas needing attention. Maybe you're overweight or stressed out. Do you fuel your days with caffeine and take-out food? Could it be you're overdue for a checkup with your dentist, internist, or eye doctor?

Be sure a few of your health concerns make it into the Managed Goals Workshop. Without our health, we have nothing. You know this all too well if you've had a health scare or suffer from a chronic condition. You're lucky if this seems like just another platitude, but someday its meaning will be crystal clear. Don't wait for that day or fall prey to the mindset of "That won't happen to me." Just like everything else relating to personal success and wellness, good health involves awareness (no denial here) and consistently good choices.

My Top Suggestions:

In addition to the list of goals that results from your Personal Reboot, I offer three suggestions that every exceptional leader will benefit from. In my practice as a health coach, my clients, without exception, need reinforcement in at least one of the following areas. Even though my suggestions are undeniably basic—the first two you've surely heard hundreds of times—they bear repeating because they allow for the strongest, healthiest, and most robust platform from which all or your energy, ideas, and talents as a leader flow.

Sleep

Adequate sleep is elusive to many of us, especially as leaders. Two reasons seem to be at the root. The first is that many go-getters don't have much time for sleep. A full night's sleep is seen as a luxury, one that that many successful people deny themselves. We've all heard about movers and shakers who require only about four hours a night (think Martha Stewart, Bill Clinton, Barak Obama, and Donald Trump). Remember, these folks are anomalies. They represent only one to three percent of the population. If you're not regularly logging between seven and nine hours—and one-third of us sleep fewer than six hours each night—you're accumulating a sleep debt that has far-reaching negative effects on the body and mind.

The second reason we don't get enough shuteye is that many of us fall into a cycle of bad habits that undermine our ability to get a sound night's sleep. Poor sleep quality is often blamed on age or chalked up to stress, but there are ways to improve our sleep.

The first step in improving sleep is to understand why it's so important to our health and our overall success. Our bodies contain a delicate mix of biochemical, which regulate how we feel and behave. These brain chemicals become depleted throughout the day, particularly by stress. Our bodies restore this important balance through sleep.

- Mentally, sleep deprivation makes us more forgetful, less able to process new information, and leaves us vulnerable to depression and anxiety. More sleep keeps cortisol (the stress hormone) in check while boosting our natural mood enhancer, serotonin.

- Insufficient sleep lowers cortisol and leptin, making us more likely to crave and overindulge in fatty, crispy, salty, and sweet comfort foods.

- Physically, sleep debt highjacks our immune systems, raising the risk of hypertension and heart disease, diabetes, some cancers, and stroke.

Now that you're convinced of the fundamental importance of a good night sleep, there are a few things you can do to help you get it.

- Charge electronic devices outside of the bedroom, or completely silence them. Beeps, hums, and chirps are disruptive.

- Cover as many of the light sources in your bedroom as possible– that red light on the TV (a piece of black tape), the glow from your alarm clock (turn it around), the streetlight streaming in past your shades (invest in better window treatments).

- Kennel your pets at night or have them sleep outside of your bedroom. I know it sounds hard-hearted, but as comforting and sweet as they are, they wake us up a lot. We need lengthy periods of deep sleep that aren't possible if we're repeatedly awakened by our furry bedmates.

- Have a bedtime routine that doesn't involve electronics. At least a half hour before bed, dim the lights, step away from the computer, turn off the TV, and do something quiet and relaxing. Make this a habit so that your body comes to know the signals that sleep is imminent.

If you wake at night and have trouble getting back to sleep:

- Take a look at your exercise level during the day. Is your mind worn out, but your body under exercised?

- Are you anxious about a problem or upcoming event? Keep a pen and paper next to your bed and take five to ten minutes to jot down ideas, to-dos, even worries. The simple act of putting them on paper will help you rest more easily.

- Is heartburn an issue? Try eating dinner earlier. Elevate your head and shoulders while you sleep, and avoid foods that trigger indigestion. If that doesn't help, see your doctor.

- If you drink alcohol, resist the urge to have a nightcap. Wine or whiskey may help you nod off faster, but as the alcohol is metabolized, it becomes harder to stay asleep and sleep well.

- Are your mattress, sheets, pillows, and PJs comfortable? How's the temperature in the bedroom?

Most people don't realize they're sleep-deprived. They don't tie their irritability, lack of self-discipline, or difficulty concentrating to sleep debt. I recommend that you try some of the suggestions above and take notice of other changes that result.

More Fresh Fruits and Vegetables

It's not news that fruits and vegetables are healthy, but I have a strategy for anyone trying to improve his or her eating habits. Don't spend energy counting calories. Forget about denying yourself certain foods. Banish the word *diet* from your vocabulary. Simply eat more fruits and vegetables. By eating more fiber-rich, vitamin-packed fresh produce, you will be crowding out some of the less healthy choices in your day. Keep in mind you can enjoy an enormous vegetable-laden salad and not come close to the fat and calories in a burger and fries. And since we're not denying ourselves, go ahead and have a few fries; chances are you won't want nearly as many.

Go for variety. Try new things. If your taste buds are somewhat challenged at the thought of veggies, set a goal of trying at least one new fruit or vegetable each day for a week. Another helpful "rule" is to limit any after-dinner snacking to fruit only. You'll be surprised at the awareness this raises around the difference between true hunger and a craving for something sweet.

Fruits and vegetables are also nature's best source for vitamins and minerals. Increasing your intake will provide your body with more of the nutrients necessary for robust health. When you consider everything you put in your mouth as opportunity to nourish your body, you'll eat more mindfully and be less likely to use food for comfort.

Less Sitting

My third suggestion isn't quite as obvious as sleeping more and eating better, but being sedentary for long periods of time is somewhat of an epidemic, especially among those working in mid- to upper-level jobs. We tend to sit in long meetings, travel by air and car frequently, and plant ourselves in front of the computer for hours on end. On average, Americans are seated for nine hours each day! In 2013, the American Heart Association stated that too much sitting is as dangerous to our health as smoking.

Even regular exercise won't offset the negative impact of sitting for long periods of time. What does help is incremental movements throughout the day, something Mayo Clinic physician, J.A. Levine, has termed NEAT (non-exercise activity thermogenesis). NEAT encompasses any energy expended throughout the day—from sleeping to fidgeting to climbing stairs—that is not done for exercise. Levine and others have found these activities add up and have a significant impact on our metabolic rate.

Be more mindful about the length of time you spend sitting still. When doing computer work, set a reminder on your phone to stand and stretch every 15 or 30 minutes. Take the stairs all the time. Consider scheduling a walking meeting as opposed to discussing business over lunch. When on a conference call, put on your headset and pace around the room. You can even add in some deep knee bends, and no one on the call will be the wiser.

Wearing a pedometer or using a smart phone app to track your movements is hands down the best way to track your movement. Leaders know you manage what you measure, so why not measure your daily activities in order to increase them?

Standing desks or treadmill desks are becoming more common in the workplace. Some companies invest in one or two, allowing employees to rotate through the workstation throughout the day. Certainly, investing in the health of your employees is a remarkable way to gain their trust and respect.

Your Reach as a Leader Includes Creating a Wellness Culture

As much as you endeavor to improve your health and habits for yourself and your personal success, remember that as a leader you set the tone for many others. In the lingo of positive psychology, you're an "influencer." By practicing and embodying good self-care habits, you inspire those around you. As a leader, you're in a position to model good habits, reward healthy choices, and spark constructive change. In essence, creating a culture of wellness for you and those you manage is a powerfully productive leadership skill.

A wellness culture will not take hold if leaders don't invest personally in the health-promoting ideas and tools. If it's not good enough for the boss, then the team probably won't spend the time. Employees know when a wellness program is primarily concerned with improving the bottom line through fewer absences and less expensive health insurance costs. But when a company fully supports employee wellbeing, a zeitgeist forms and builds to strengthen the company, its employees, and its leaders.

-Barclay Schraff

☑WELKnote:

Sometimes the highest-impact things you can do in your life are also the simplest.

Chapter 55 - Putting It All Together

You've done some amazing things to revitalize your mind, introducing some new ideas and looking objectively at some of your routines and priorities. Now it's time to revisit some of your previous work. Here are the recommendations:

1. Review your index cards from your energy audit. You're now in position to make some great decisions about habits and routines that may not fit into the life you want to live. Look closely at the routines that are costing you energy. For a leader, energy is the greatest asset. Without it, all of your capability and credibility have no impact. Do you want to "fire" a few of these routines? Should you eliminate one or two now and look at the rest in a few weeks?

2. Think about your neglected areas. Is it time to reintroduce something important into your life? If it is, make a formal decision about it. Actually schedule whatever it is on your calendar and add reminders wherever you need to. Strongly consider Schraff's expert recommendations on improving your overall wellness. Know this: When you move an important aspect of your life out of the "neglected" category, it can bring you a lot of satisfaction and joy. Just focus on one of these at a time, and you can always revisit your list later.

3. Let's go back to your goals list. Are you still satisfied with the twelve or fewer priority goals you decided on? If so, it's time to get some buy-in from the people who would be affected by these goals. Talk them out and get feedback. Some of your goals will be

100% individual, and these are the goals that are "by you and for you." You're really going to enjoy making them happen.

Be formal in your approach to these top-priority goals. I know people who carry them around in a special leather portfolio. Some people have them laminated. You've probably seen people who post them all over the place. Some people make them public, and some keep them resolutely private. Whatever choices you make about your goals, understand that these are your fuel for doing extraordinary things. One last question: Would it be possible for a person to have anything more valuable than their goals?

That is your Exceptional Leaders Reboot! We hope that you took the time to go through the steps or that you will at soon.

☑WELKnote:

All leader's need to shake her personal Etch-A-Sketch® every once in a while and start fresh. Absolutely amazing results can come from new commitments.

▌Conclusion

We sincerely hope that what we have shared inspires you to become a better and more capable leader. For over 25 years, we have studied and shared the passion of leadership, and we've presented you with ideas and strategies that have yielded results. We intentionally did not share *all* of our failures, as there's no way you could take the time to read them.

There's no higher calling than leadership. Leaders influence people and organizations in important and permanent ways. They're the people in our lives who help us to understand who and what we can become. They're the people who said the right thing at the right time and changed the way we looked at a certain situation, or even better, changed the course of our lives forever.

We hope this book inspires you to do that for the people you lead. The responsibility of leadership is not to be taken lightly; it can be the most pride-swallowing, gut-wrenching, time-consuming, tongue-biting job in the world. But if you do it right, it can also give a leader's life much more meaning and impact.

Now you know ... What Exceptional Leaders Know.

Tracy Spears & Wally Schmader

Thank You

There would be no way to thank everyone who helped us write this book, but here is a short list of people who strongly influenced the content and delivery of What Exceptional Leaders Know:

Cindy Bristow	Chuck Reddick
Ed & Cherie Brown	Steve Richards
Paul Buske	Lillian Russell
Arvell Craig	Justin Sachs
Stephen Dobie	Marla Sanchez
Gordon Dunn	Barclay Schraff
Ken Eissing	Amanda Smith
Donna Hathaway	Jim Stovall
Marita Hynes	Carolyn Vanhauen
Don Jones	Oprah Winfrey
June Penick Miller	Jane Wiseman
Mary Miscisin	Barney Zeng
Mercy Pilkington	John Zimmerman

Additional Resources

Tracy Spears and Wally Schmader are engaged in many leadership-focused projects including:

- Executive Coaching
- Keynote Speaking
- Leadership Training
- Corporate Retreat Programs
- Organizational Leadership Coaching & Training

Tracy Spears has specialized programs focused on:

- Temperament Training & Coaching
- Leadership Temperament Fluency
- Diversity & Inclusion Training
- Sales Training
- Healthcare practice management
- Employee Engagement
- Stress Management

Wally Schmader has specialized programs focused on:

- Sales Training
- Executive Leadership Coaching
- Group Leadership Programs
- Sales Leadership Programs
- Virtual Transition Coaching
- Leadership Development Programs

Tracy and Wally can both be reached at
information@thewelkgroup.com

or individually at
tracy@thewelkgroup.com
and
wally@thewelkgroup.com

Information can also be found at their website:
www.whatexceptionalleadersknow.com

☑WELKnotes:

☑ Your reputation is your brand. It is one of your most valuable assets. Protect it.

☑ Genuine humility is the most attractive leadership personality trait … and it can be learned.

☑ Leaders must actively defend themselves against obsolescence.

☑ Exceptional leaders are constantly reinventing themselves … they do not coast.

☑ Stress is going to be part of every leader's job. Understanding where it comes from and how to mange it is a key step in becoming an exceptional leader.

☑ Don't let the influence of data and consensus-building shrink the importance of communicating and inspiring your team. People want purpose and passion.

☑ It can be hard to maintain a healthy level of self awareness as a leader, especially as you move higher in your organization.

☑ Purposeful self improvement is the cornerstone of exceptional leadership.

☑ Even experienced leaders can easily fall into a rut if they do not intentionally challenge themselves to grow.

☑ Leaders sometimes need to make deliberate changes in the way they do things.

☑ Routines and habits are two of the most powerful forces in your life. Leverage them to create the outcomes you want.

☑ High performance leaders have advisors and mentors. They learn to aggregate and leverage the best advice and best examples they can find.

☑ Aspiration and ambition will provide the fuel you need to accomplish your objectives as a leader.

☑ Keep yourself open to new ideas. Be ready and able to change your mind about things. Welcome the people and ideas that challenge your point of view.

☑ The ability to manage your priorities and energy within the constraints of time is the master skill of success. Audit how you are spending your time and energy assets.

☑ Consistent self improvement is a must for today's progressive leaders.

☑ You become what you think about. Are your thoughts helping or hurting you as a leader?

☑ Leaders should be measured by their ability to influence performance and produce results.

☑ It is the leaders' primary responsibility to get their people in position to succeed in their roles.

☑ Take the time to reevaluate and rediscover the people on your team ... and maybe you need to try Brussels sprouts again.

☑ Exceptional leaders understand the need to manage both the environment and the people.

☑ High-performance organizations create an expectation of success.

☑ Nothing highlights a leader's strengths and weaknesses like a promotion.

☑ The best leaders do not leave performance to chance. Be decisive in your actions. It is your responsibility to make people better or make room for someone new.

☑ Exceptional leaders look for big and small opportunities to enhance their employees' work experience.

☑ There are a multitude of meaningful ways for leaders to inspire their people.

☑ Exceptional leaders have to learn how to coach effectively and how to recognize progress when they see it.

☑ The ability to be direct and ask the right questions is another cornerstone trait for exceptional leaders.

☑ Leaders are in the expectations business; they learn to see the upside in people and situations.

☑ Leaders understand that there are many ways for people to contribute and make the effort to recognize as many of them as possible.

☑ Understanding your personal interaction style, whether you are extroverted or introverted, is a big step in being an effective leader.

☑ Introverted leaders understand that they need to schedule personal time to preserve and renew their energy.

☑ Extroverted leaders understand that they need to pause to make room for others in the conversation.

☑ Sometimes you don't know what you don't know.

☑ Temperament fluency gives leaders an understanding and appreciation of the gifts and perspectives of the people they serve.

☑ Temperament Fluency enables the leader to understand what motivates each person they serve.

☑ The steps for learning temperament fluency are the same as the steps for learning anything else. It is a study and requires awareness, commitment and practice

☑ Exceptional leaders understand that their greatest conflicts and challenges will typically come from people whose dominant temperaments are their own least-developed temperaments.

☑ To put it as simply as possible, effective leadership is the ability to influence people toward a common objective.

☑ Exceptional Leaders have the ability to provide a "jolt" to their people in the right way at the right time.

☑ Effective leaders understand that trust is something they earn over time, and without it, their possibilities will be drastically limited.

☑ The Exceptional Leader will do whatever it takes to build and demonstrate trust in their people.

☑ Pay special attention to anything in your business that seems to run on its own momentum. Often, the usefulness of an idea or event runs out long before it is actually ended.

☑ Exceptional Leaders understand the transformative power of appreciation and recognition.

☑ Smart leaders recognize setbacks as a necessary part of growth. The know how to plan for and manage those situations ... leading their teams to greater success.

☑ Exceptional Leaders know how to leverage many different strategies to drive results. They understand that different situations call for varying approaches.

☑ Sometimes the most effective thing a leader can do is to get out of the way and let people produce.

☑ Exceptional Leaders know that sustainable growth comes only from developing people through focused coaching and the investment of time and attention.

☑ Being an absolute "truth teller" should be a non-negotiable part of an exceptional leader's character.

☑ Sometimes "right now" is the best time to get started.

☑ Knowing and understanding where you are spending your energy will allow any leader to preserve that energy for the most important parts of their lives.

☑ The most successful leaders start with goals and go confidently forward from there.

☑ Sometimes the highest-impact things you can do in your life are also the simplest.

☑ Every leader needs to shake her personal Etch-A-Sketch® every once in a while and start fresh. Absolutely amazing results can come from new commitments.

Notes:

_____

_____

_____

_____

_____

_____

_____

_____

_____

_____

_____

_____

_____

_____

_____

_____

_____

_____

_____

_____

_____

_____

_____

_____

_____

_____

_____

_____

CPSIA information can be obtained at www.ICGtesting.com
Printed in the USA
LVOW10s0008081114

412624LV00001B/1/P